Tall Tales of a BIG GOD

Tall Tales of a BIG GOD

WORD PUBLISHING
Nelson Word Ltd
Milton Keynes, England
WORD AUSTRALIA
Kilsyth, Australia
NELSON WORD CANADA
Vancouver, B.C., Canada
STRUIK CHRISTIAN BOOKS (PTY) LTD
Cape Town, South Africa
JOINT DISTRIBUTORS SINGAPORE –
ALBY COMMERCIAL ENTERPRISES PTE LTD
and
CAMPUS CRUSADE, ASIA LTD
PHILIPPINE CAMPUS CRUSADE FOR CHRIST
Quezon City, Philippines
CHRISTIAN MARKETING NEW ZEALAND LTD
Havelock North, New Zealand
JENSCO LTD
Hong Kong
SALVATION BOOK CENTRE
Malaysia

TALL TALES OF A BIG GOD

Contents

'Perhaps the mission of those who love mankind is to make people laugh at the truth, to make truth laugh, because the only truth lies in learning to free ourselves from insane passion for the truth.'

Umberto Eco

'Systems of explanation illuminate up to a point and then falsify. And when the attempt is made to gather up the totality of man's experience of God within the confines of some systematic orthodoxy, then the falsification can be considerable.'

H. A. Williams

Introduction

One hundred and one things happen to me. Some say I am accident prone. I do know I have always been a storyteller and have dripped on continuously for the best part of a lifetime.

So here are one hundred and one or more short stories that I have experienced or encountered in my quest for life so far. They are selected from the religious side of life—if that can ever be separated from the secular—and are meant to provoke us to take ourselves less seriously and maybe even present the image that to love God and enjoy yourself are not incompatible. Hopefully they may even help us to debunk a little self-righteousness, perhaps to get away from rules and regulations for a change and back on the road of grace. Well, that's a tall order!

If you recognise yourself anywhere in them please extend me the courtesy of forgiveness and allow that with the passage of time they are by now quite loosely based on truth. Some of my friends say they have heard my stories a dozen times or more—and they get better every time!

My heartfelt thanks to Eileen who has weathered many of these stories first hand and been the wind beneath my wings for forty-five years; to Phil Streeter, Dave Bryant, Bridget Boyle, Shirley Wing and Alan

Halden, whose sense of humour has always been an inspiration and a blessing (religious word meaning to invoke happiness).

So off you go, to delve into the sweepings from the church's cutting room floor, all hopefully salvaged by The Director.

Happy reading.

Maurice Smith
November 1992

Our Chains Stayed On . . .

'Loyalty to petrified opinion never yet broke a chain or freed a human soul.'

Mark Twain

'Man is born to be free, but everywhere he is in chains.'

Jean Jacques Rousseau

'If I have a vivid spiritual experience and have power over people by means of that experience, the danger is that I usurp the place of God and say, "You must come my way; you must have this experience." This may damage you but it damages me even more, because my spirit is far removed from the spirit of Jesus Christ, it is the spirit of the spiritual prig.'

Oswald Chambers

Except You Become as Little Children

Perhaps the earliest memory of any religious activity was attending the Band of Hope which was a local temperance society dedicated to keeping us seven-year-olds off drink for life. I am sure I never understood what was the purpose of it all, but we played games in the hall and they gave out real medals for attendance, so that was a draw.

Much later in life I remember having difficulty reconciling a temperance meeting that always stressed total abstinence—if you catch my drift! I like to think now that I am truly temperate as I only swig the occasional jar or two. Back in my youth the Band of Hope gave way to other spheres of searching.

The next abortive attempt to soar into the realms of youthful spirituality was energised by the dubious motive of jealousy. A schoolboy pal of mine came home from the Salvation Army proudly displaying a gleaming silver trumpet, with which he would blast one repetitive note from his back bedroom window, to the intense annoyance of all the neighbours. I just had to have one!

Unfortunately the local 'Sally Army' (as we called the uniformed preachers with their *War Cry* magazines) was not merely a benevolent society and required my attendance at meetings before they would part with any hardware. My first intrepid appearance was a frightening affair, for I can still remember vividly the bonneted old lady who suddenly stood to her feet in the middle of the service, pointed to the ceiling and shrieked, 'When I die, I want to go . . . Up there! Up there!'

I was puzzled and stared in childlike curiosity at the gallery, wondering what secret delights could be hidden 'up there' so that an old lady would want to spend eternity exploring among the gloomy benches. On returning home my parents patiently explained that she must have been pointing to heaven, somewhere beyond the balcony. Detail of the afterlife has always been a bit of a mystery to me, I am nowhere near as clear as some. Maybe the confusion originated way back there in a spartan citadel on the north side of the River Thames?

Not only did we have to qualify by attending services indoors, but we were also required to march in my neighbourhood, then stand in a circle in the middle of the road to sing and shout out testimonies. Thankfully there was very little motor traffic in those days, but will I ever forget the piles of steaming horse manure? I used to stare down at the road surface and hope—or perhaps even pray?—that none of my mates would pass by and start to jeer. What I did for that trumpet!

But I never got it. When it came to my turn to be musically encouraged they had exhausted the supply of full instruments and issued me with a mere mouthpiece with which to practise. In spite of pursed lips and bursting lungs all I could ever muster was a rude sounding raspberry. Needless to say I gave up that particular pursuit of holiness and resigned in an ungodly huff.

Thirty years passed before a friend of mine took me to an 'Army' meeting once again, this time to accompany him as the invited speaker from the nearby Honor Oak Fellowship. We did not do well again I am afraid, for being ignorant of the sacredness with which some of the furniture was held, we parked our overcoats on the Mercy Seat.

Maybe I was meant to confine my activities to supporting the charity envelopes and admiring their work among the destitute, both of which I gladly do to this day.

Schoolboy Chorister

I have always liked singing and with many others think I am much better than Bing Crosby (if you remember him)—but in the bath, of course. My membership of a North London Anglican choir was established before I got out of short trousers. My friends and I spent most of the service ducked down behind the choir stalls playing word games with our shoes off, until called to leave in formal procession swamped in ageing surplices and cassocks. On occasion it was known for us to depart unshod when we were caught unawares with a hurried final hymn and blessing.

I was unceremoniously dismissed this choir for laughing out loud during matins. It was excusable really. The vicar appeared so absurd as he read soberly from the Prophet Isaiah, informing the disinterested congregation that certain men were 'those who sat upon a wall eating their own dung and drinking their own piss!' I am sure there must have been a more suitable reading somewhere in the Good Book, or a better translation.

My departure was with little regret except the loss of my pocket money, and I proposed never to meet up with that particular man of God again.

It was a false proposition. More than ten years later as a subaltern in *mufti* just leaving the service, I attended his marriage instruction classes at the Rectory. Now well gone seventy years this man of doubtful holy orders made a bold attempt to fondle my future wife—on my blind side, of course. Some instruction!

On the nuptial day the poor man nearly got his come-uppance. He all but choked on alcohol fumes as I swayed before him during the ceremony. His eyes bulged with disbelief as he stepped back out of range of my breath whilst beholding the pips and ribbons on my dress uniform. I stood tall.

Who would ever have thought that such a young urchin would aspire to a King's Commission?

Ah, but it's a strange life. Who would ever have thought that such an irreverent choirboy would aspire to love the Lord his God with all his heart, soul, mind and strength. Yet, so it proved.

I've also grown old enough to know that maybe the vicar aspired too, in his own way. He just had one or two problems that's all.

But then, who hasn't?

Handel's Lullaby

There are times when the worshippers' eyes are closed in more than meditation or embarrassment. Folk have been known to go to sleep.

The most flagrant case I know of happened in a Baptist Church in Bristol during the Christmas rendering of that masterly but lengthy classic, Handel's *Messiah*.

It was well known that the Minister and the Choir Master did not hit it off. Hence no one was surprised when the introduction was decidedly frosty. After this the minister, whose pulpit was raised the usual ten feet above contradiction, sank down out of sight as the choirmaster raised his arms and the choir stood. They were situated in the balcony a further five feet higher and to the minister's left. The stage was set.

At the eventual ending of the rendition the performers sat and everyone duly waited for the minister to stand and say a customary few words of thanks. He did not appear and not a man moved . . . for at least five minutes.

The Choir Master then leaned over as far as he dared, whilst every eye down below swivelled surreptitiously to follow his action. He sank back obviously unsatisfied and the silence continued.

A further few minutes elapsed before he risked another dangerous lean out, but it was evident to all that he could not quite see over the high cloth sides of the minister's booth. Titters were now beginning to break out, but still no leadership was asserted.

Finally, there was a stirring from within the secret

place and a Chad-like pair of eyes peered over the brim to reconnoitre the scene and were then slowly lowered. After a few seconds there followed a loud throat clearing from deep within the structure and the ministerial culprit confidently stood, upright and unabashed, to thank the choir as if nothing untoward had happened.

Did he have any idea he had dropped off? Was he brazening it out? Your guess is as good as mine. Yet once more I was left with more of those nagging growing questions concerning this game called 'Churches and Chapels'.

'Would Jesus have joined in the game? Was insecurity at the base of the petrified inactivity? Do we sometimes leave reality at the door in exchange for our hymn sheet or psalter?' On these I pondered.

The Adult Village Choir

When I was twenty-six we opted for the countryside and went to live at Kingham, a large village in the Cotswolds. It was there I had my black and white conversion. I was keen.

No sooner had I put in an appearance at church than the rector noticed my powerful vocal contribution and suggested I join the choir. Of course I informed him I could not read music, but apparently this was no hindrance. 'We're all one happy family,' he assured me, 'You'll be fine!'

I duly turned up at the village hall the next Tuesday for practice. The phone had rung just before I left, which made me a little late. When I entered it was to find no kindly vicar present, but a robust dragon of a lady who looked up and snorted as I entered.

'What are you?' she demanded, looking over the top of her horn rims.

I said I did not understand.

'What are you? What part do you sing?'

I said I didn't know.

'You don't know! You don't know! . . . Join Mr Partridge over there.'

If the rector had walked in I could have cheerfully killed him. However, Bill Partridge was my friendly local insurance agent, so I took comfort in the fact that he would see me through somehow.

'Mr Partridge is the only tenor tonight,' she stated, 'You can join him.'

With that she handed me a sheet of music and motioned me to a seat.

This awesome creature then announced that we should all stand and sing the first anthem; music which, of course, I had never heard before.

I really did try my best. I moved my head up and down as I read along the score and hoped the notes would follow along. Of course I was not even sure I was singing the tenor score.

Suddenly there was a scream from the front,

'Stop! Stop! It is dreadful. Dreadful!'

We were then all instructed to sing our parts separately. Oh dear!

I whispered to friend Partridge that I could not read music.

He replied, neither could he.

Only two tenors and neither of us could read the score!

After one or two other sections had satisfactorily sung their parts she called on us.

We stood meekly and began to protest weakly,

'. . . I am afraid . . .'

'Nonsense!' she insisted, 'sing up!'

Well, we tried.

I was trying to follow Mr P and he was trying to follow me.

We sang slowly and I could hear that it sounded quite terrible.

At this juncture the tittering began to break out.

More screaming came from the front,

'Stop!! Stop!!'

'But The Reverend said it didn't matter if we couldn't read music . . .'

'Didn't matter? That is ridiculous. I'll speak to the Rector!'

The place was by now in uproar.

To be honest, I can't remember how it all ended, but I do know I never went again. For years I nursed the hope that woman would never get through heaven's gates, for I certainly did not want to spend eternity in her company.

Both tenors did try to explain to the Rector; but he kept pouring oil on troubled waters, stuck to his principle of no confrontation and kept the jobs filled.

Are You Comprehensively Covered?

It seems to me that all ritual contains great potential for the absurd. What levels of ludicrous behaviour have we sunk to at times in the name of piety?

How can we fail to smile, looking back to the Minister's severe wife handing out a varied assortment of sober hats at the back of an East London chapel, before the female of the species are allowed to enter?

Topping this, no doubt, was the impromptu prayer-meeting that took us all by surprise, so that the ladies had no 'head covering' with them. Imagine my incredulity to find one dear soul digging into her handbag for a paper bag, whilst another conjured up the plastic variety from somewhere in the depths. There they sat for best part of two hours with these ridiculous appendages perched on their heads.

I was not present, but have it on good authority that some North London Brethren Assembly ladies have even been seen sporting crash helmets because no other form of covering was available. ('Heads should be covered because of the angels,' St Paul wrote.) Perhaps these oh-so-proper ladies thought they were about to be stoned from on high for impropriety?

Anyway, those one-hundred-and-ten commandments of the New Testament were issued two thousand years ago and there were possibly good moral and cultural reasons for such exhortations then. We can at least give those early church leaders the benefit of the doubt.

Today all this foolhardiness is liable to continue and

increase whilst literalism abounds and we insist upon trying to outdo Jesus and the apostles in their level of supposed piety.

One of the men who affected my life more than any in those early days of ritualism, insisted that once 'the sisters' saw the real principle of submission, they would willingly wear a dozen hats on their heads. Unfortunately I am unable to truthfully record that I ever saw anyone take his solemn exhortation literally.

If the Good Book stated 'He rose up early that morning to pray', then we assumed we should get up every morning early to do likewise. Whereas it may well be that He usually had a lie-in, and this occasion was specifically stated because it was the exception!

Well, why not?

He was human enough on many other occasions. Perhaps too human for us?

In the Floral Dance

Not all foolishness takes place on our own doorstep thank goodness. Some of the most incredible things I have seen and heard took place when the family were on holiday in the West Country.

It was Tuesday evening in lazy Port Isaac on the North Cornish Coast, where year by year I had ministered at the little guest house overlooking the sea. The entire holiday was idyllic and the ministry wasn't bad either.

Tuesday nights were always a bit different.

The brass band played for a while by the harbour and then struck up the familiar Floral Dance, which was the signal for hundreds of holiday makers and locals to link arms and dance. The surging mass then snaked its way up the narrow High Street, singing as best they could, whilst puffing hard at the steep gradient and desperately trying to maintain the continuous one-two-three-hop of the Cornish speciality dance.

There was simply no point in starting our meeting on time as the brass band effectively brought everything to a halt as it passed close by the seafront windows, turning fifty yards on at the blind end for the return journey. The guesthouse had more than its fair share of the free entertainment. So I delayed the start and went down to the quayside.

At the foot of the hill I joined the dancers and puffed my way up to the top and along the promenade. It was great fun. As we jostled past the guesthouse I peeled off and danced my happy one-two-three-hop up the path and into the lounge.

'Here comes our carnal brother!' remarked one of the

guests, with only the hint of a smile and leaving us all wondering how jocular the remark was really meant to be.

Later I spoke to the house owner, 'Was that remark half-serious?' I queried, finding it hard to believe anyone could be so muddled in their thinking as to confuse a floral dance on a summer's evening with carnality.

'Oh, that is nothing,' he replied, and began to explain that when you have religious people around, anything that interferes with their services or their Bible study can quite easily be categorised as carnality.

I shuddered with disbelief which encouraged him to explain further.

'That brass band can really annoy some people,' he continued. 'One year we had a lady who was so irate at the interruption that she rushed out to witness to them.'

'This is sheer madness,' I thought.

The owner continued, 'Apparently the band was so loud she could not make herself heard. As she re-entered the lounge several people enquired if she had managed to make contact at all. The budding evangelist then proudly informed everyone that it had been too noisy for conversation, ". . . however I did manage to poke a tract down one man's trombone!" '

I screamed with laughter at the thought.

But what has it come to? How low have we sunk?

Instead of folk following us around, as they followed Jesus around wanting to know the secret of His lifestyle we have completely turned the tables. What are we doing desperately chasing about after folk, like salesmen trying to make their weekly targets?

Perhaps we had better learn to live more attractive lives before we pass on our purported Good News. We certainly do not want to convert people in order that they might be as miserable as the central character of this anecdote.

Anyway, it is rude to give people answers to questions they are not asking!

Anglican Bells

The same friendly picturesque port with its white-washed cottages and tiny church almost toppling into the sea, played host to one of the saltiest stories I have the pleasure to recall.

So I heard on arrival, the new vicar had been distinctly unimpressed by the tinkling bell atop his miniature church. Apparently the offending hollow vessel had regularly, if somewhat weakly, summoned a tiny band of the faithful to their corporate worship since time immemorial. 'Tinklebell' had a place of affection in the hearts of many locals.

No matter. It would have to go!

The problem was solved when His Reverence acquired a tape recording of magnificent cathedral bells. It was arranged, by means of amplification in the belfry, for these to peal forth both loud and long upon every sabbath morn.

The result was incongruous to say the least, and also caused the irate locals and holidaymakers alike to lose hours of sleep. The ecstasy of a Sunday morning lie-in—so vital perhaps after the heady Saturday night carousals—was a thing of the past.

In spite of many representations from the community the new vicar steadfastly refused to revert to the time-honoured local bell.

Youth so often has its own way of dealing with situations like this. And so it proved in would-be sleepy Port Isaac. For in the still of the night, some of the most enterprising opposition broke in and substituted the tape and altered the timing mechanism.

What delight fills my soul every time I let my imagination run amok, knowing as I do that every house in the whole community had a door or window that was thrust wide open with indignation, when (at the distinctly ungodly hour of two-thirty a.m.) the Beatles screamed loud into the night air, 'It's been a hard day's night!'

I have it on the good authority of my own first-hand experience, that Tinklebell now once more inoffensively makes its request to those who have ears to hear. The others sleep on. Undisturbed.

Most of us learn the hard way, don't we?

On the QT

Many chains were bound on my life soon after my Christian conversion.

I started off by enjoying the upsurge of life from within, but those with greater experience told me there were also rules and regulations imposed from without; 'divine principles' they called these.

One of the very first was confided by a solid evangelical gentleman from nearby Chipping Norton, who asked if I was having a QT.

'What's that?' I queried.

I was informed it was a 'Quiet Time' in the morning to start the day right. I tried to say everything was all right, God was with me; but it was to no avail. I needed this special QT.

'You must have one of these every day, to keep close to God!'

I endeavoured to protest, but apparently I did not understand.

Then I was told by another Bible-puncher that Billy Graham read three psalms and five proverbs every day, and should I do less?

So the list of do's and don'ts went on, until I became a very miserable offender indeed.

Why did I listen? Out of respect, I guess.

It was to be years before I learned what nonsense this all was and started living from the bottom line inside of me that had been such a blessing at the very outset.

I treasure my own conversion experience, but I do not demand that everyone has to have a similar experience or walk the same path as me in order to be right with God. Such tolerance took years to come, once I had been indoctrinated by those who felt they had some special hold on the truth.

Now I am very wary of those with their special this and special that.

God be merciful to us who have shackled each other.

Sheep or Goats?

I suppose I did my best to conform.

Just short of thirty years of age and I got myself sprinkled with baptismal water with my best friend, a young man five years my junior standing in as my godfather.

Then I was confirmed by the Bishop of Oxford the same evening; but by now I was beginning to feel very confused indeed. I stood in line behind a gaggle of giggling girls who were pinching each other's bottoms. And I was making decisions of such immense·importance!

I attended Parochial Church Council meetings, but at these I witnessed my new friend the Rector behaving like a peacekeeper, not a peacemaker. There seemed a world of difference to me. Perhaps he was not cut out to be a priest after all? He had liberal amounts of oil to pour in every direction and I felt a million miles removed from the company of the earthy reality of those rugged fishermen who had walked the dusty roads with Jesus. I felt more as though I had joined a knitting circle.

Frustration was gradually pulling me down.

Next I tried my hand at the local Bible study, but there I found my frank questions and opinions were not what was expected. I remember causing quite an uproar when I stated that I felt the Apostle Paul was a hypocrite. Apparently I was not supposed to say things like that.

One night the headmaster of a local public school grabbed hold of me in the dark village street after a gruesome PCC meeting where much had been swept under the carpet. Sensing my growing desperation, he spoke starkly.

'If God ever calls you to preach young man, remember He said, "Feed my sheep", he did not say "Tickle the ears of the goats!" '

I felt He would never ask me to preach anything; I was a greenhorn and needed to learn so much. It was a big new world.

Nearly forty years later I have finally admitted that many people prefer to have their ears tickled.

Scrabble—That's All

There are so many areas in which leadership is held in unwarranted awe and it is exposed in the simplicities of everyday life. I vividly remember playing a renowned word game, Scrabble, with a quiet sensitive young lady who was known to be quite an expert. I was certainly not an expert and it was also my first game for many years. However, nearing completion the scores were almost level and I was extremely pleased with myself.

Gradually, a sinking feeling engulfed me as I began to realise I had been manoeuvred into retaining all the awkward high-scoring letters. My rack was crammed with them. What could I do with a Q without a U? Not to mention a confounded X that had absolutely nowhere to go. And they were just a couple of examples!

I should never have been talked into playing the silly game in the first place. I have always been a bad loser and this night was proving no exception.

A sullen mood swept over me, and whereas I had been playing quickly and confidently, now I had ground almost to a standstill. Finally I became paralysed into total inactivity. I desperately tried to smile, but my attitude was out of step with my face muscles. My absurd inner blackness engulfed the room as I peeped at my partner through my fingers. What I saw I shall never forget, for my young innocent partner was covered with obvious embarrassment. It was really much more than that, she was actually sending off guilt vibes that were richoteting around the whole lounge.

It was with horror that I realised the true situation.

Having sensed the dreadful atmosphere in the room—who could miss it?—she had concluded it could not possibly be emanating from me, as I was an older man, a senior leader and much too spiritually advanced for such behaviour. It was a short step from here to deciding that somehow she must be in the wrong. Given the choice between herself and me, it was obvious to her conditioned mind that only she could be at fault.

I gulped and swallowed any pride that remained, then did my best to convince the oversensitised conscience before me that the whole thing was my fault. I was just a bad loser, that was the end of it! I said. But I wonder if she believes me to this day.

When will we learn that there should be no inequality among us, and that the possession of a gift does not bring elevation in rank? I am fully persuaded that the presence of hierarchy diverts the common eye from the lowly One, who himself took a towel and served to the end. Surely the last thing we want is to lose sight of Him.

A Wag in the Church

Much religion is merely semantics I am sure. Gareth brought this home to me.

Running stride for stride one evening along with our local club, the *Romford Roadents* he asked me, 'What really is the difference between "unlawful" and "illegal"?' This because I was known as some kind of expert on the matter of Christian law and grace.

I hopped all around the subject without being definitive. As the pace was slow, the whole pack got drawn into offering their views. The debate lasted for the whole five miles and we were all completely knotted up with frustration by the time we reached home base.

Under group pressure Gareth eventually conceded that he had come to some conclusion himself, but was not sure if it was right.

Under further pressure he admitted that he felt:

'Perhaps unlawful meant one would be breaking the law, whilst ill-egal was probably . . . . a sick bird!'

Everyone was furious and some were also amused. But one policeman still insisted there was a difference between illegal and unlawful . . .

Bingo!

How often the church is the butt of humour.

Donald was always one for a laugh. Arriving at his wedding reception in the Anglican church hall he noticed that there was a Bingo session to be held that evening in the same premises. Just before his speech he excused himself for a few moments, then returned to address the wedding breakfast, a battered trilby on his head with the brim turned up all round and an improvised clerical collar round his neck.

The first words of his speech were sung in reverent tones, 'Eyes dow-own for a fu-ull house!'

Everyone collapsed with laughter; except his new wife who was quite angry. Perhaps she feared for a lifetime of this mocking hilarity.

The irony is he is a *bona fide* parson himself today, and I am sure is big enough to bear with me saying that at times he is quite parsonical too! Perhaps he does not sustain the church funds with Bingo, but thankfully he can still raise a laugh.

True Tales of False Teeth (1)

I was visiting a small house meeting attached to the Evangelical Free Church at Gallows Corner in Essex. Whilst waiting to give the message several youngsters began to ask me questions of an intense spiritual nature, to which I attended with the due sobriety and deference of someone who was supposed to know it all.

Meanwhile we munched on a tea-time snack.

Ignoring my long-departed mother's admonitions, I was talking and eating at the same time. Suddenly I realised that my mouth was full of rough-edged pieces of something very hard.

I endlessly manoeuvred the painful mess around as best I could while still trying to give life-changing answers to the eager young people.

Finally the truth dawned. I had managed to break my small denture clean in half.

Unreality of course immediately sprang to the fore and I tried to pretend nothing untoward had happened, but answering questions with a mouthful of ham roll and bits of false teeth with mustard eventually rendered me speechless and in dire danger of choking.

I was forced to make an ignominious withdrawal to the downstairs lobby in order to sort out the pieces.

When I returned to give the inspiring message, it was with two prominent gaps which I tried to cover by the alternate ploys of speaking like a ventriloquist and keeping my hand in front of my mouth.

It was unwise. The idiotic performance seemed to

hold everyone's rapt attention far more than what I was actually saying.

At least that is how I felt.

One word of honest admission would have got the matter settled and lessened the intrigue; but that would have been asking too much.

False Teeth (2)

I was still game, but outdoors this time and preaching on a box at the Canterbury cattle market. The Saturday morning entertainment included yours truly shouting at full strength to compete with the experienced market traders.

Today I cringe when I hear some eager convert doing a pale imitation of John the Baptist or John Wesley and so clearly without the attendant conviction that either brought. My wife reminds me when I am tempted to deride or interrupt, 'You did it once!'

And once I overdid it.

I had gathered a crowd and was bellowing at the top of my voice with both arms outstretched to indicate the immensity of God's love for a sinful world.

It was an horrific moment when I saw my teeth fly out and up.

I never was a dab hand in the infield, but on this occasion the hand of providence seemed to guide my own as with one deft movement I caught the molars in midair and carried on preaching as if nothing had happened.

Some youths at the back knew otherwise and went into loud hysterics.

Although I fought on bravely I lost the attention of my audience and retired with my pride severely injured.

Years of painfully gained maturity later, I wonder why on earth I did not have a good laugh and carry the crowd with me; but I guess had I got that sort of maturity I would not have been on the box at all!

False Teeth (3)

Now I cannot personally vouch for the truth of this story, but a trusted friend tells of the time a visiting Methodist preacher arrived in his village to take the evening service.

As was the custom, the visitor had tea with my friend's grandfather and during the meal his upper plate broke leaving him with a distinct lisp.

He insisted he could not possibly make his oration with such an impediment but grandfather calmly said there was no need to worry, he had a tray of several sterilised sets of teeth.

Although diffident the speaker made no overt enquiry, but was persuaded by the older man's confidence and the urgency of the situation into trying a few for size. Eventually a suitable plate was selected and they left for the service. Even though far from utterly comfortable the visitor managed without too much trouble other than a little soreness.

On the way home afterwards the speaker casually remarked how fortunate he was to have the incident happen whilst in the presence of a retired dentist, and could the other plate be repaired?

Grandad gently informed him he was not retired and was certainly not a dentist.

He was the village undertaker.

Ugh!

Twentieth-Century Crusaders

I was entreated to become a counsellor at the forthcoming Billy Graham film crusade in Chipping Norton. I did not like all the pat answers we were to give enquirers, but was assured it was the right way.

'If no one moves when the appeal is given then the counsellors should start to move slowly down the aisles' we were told. I weakly protested that this was perhaps a mite dishonest, but apparently the end fully justified the means and I was again persuaded to quench the little voice of disquiet inside me. I soon became a man-pleaser I suppose.

At times I did speak my mind, like the time after we had moved south and I was trying the Baptists for a change.

There were just a few of us dotted around the substantial building in a mining village south of Canterbury. It was very cold and as the minister came out of his vestry I could see the warm glow of an electric fire inside. He ascended into a high pulpit and started speaking down at us.

After the preliminaries I put my hand up to draw his attention. He did not look too pleased and asked me gruffly what I wanted. I said we were all very cold and could we not go and have our service in the vestry?

'Certainly not,' I was informed, '*This* is the church.'

I called back, 'No! *We* are the church, people not bricks and mortar.'

But it didn't make any difference, we still stayed out in the cold.

It was time for me to try the Methodists. They soon

told me I was what they called 'On fire for God' and should go to college to study to be a minister.

I asked if I could just share from the pulpit anyway and just like the record of the early church folk could shout out if they disagreed. But no, I needed to be ordained or at least take some proper lessons.

After a year or two I gave the whole churchgoing exercise up in despair. I dropped to my knees one night and exclaimed, 'Lord I think your Son is wonderful and your church is horrible!' You can see I was a precocious young believer.

But it was not long before a few friends and I started to form a church all of our own and that soon became as awful as the others I had left. Everyone in the church was so touchy, much more so than the folks in the pubs I had left behind.

Maybe that was a premature move of mine taking myself right out of the world like that?

Maybe that was just a bit of religion I was exercising, following others like a silly sheep, rather than listening to my own hotline to God?

Too Black and White

We in the religious minority, have always tried to avoid worldliness and many of us quite misunderstood what 'worldly' really meant anyway.

Being out of fashion with our clothes is a good example of our former absurdity. We were still in flares while every one else had changed to straights. I am not advocating being a trend-setter, rather just fitting in like JC on the mountainside, forcing John the Baptist to call out 'There stands one among you!' He was not conspicuous by being old-fashioned or outrageously trendy to help his insecurity.

A long time ago a friend of mine in Romford was chatting to the local Baptist minister on the street. In quite a natural manner he referred to something seen on TV the night before.

Imagine his astonishment when the minister seriously enquired, 'Not colour, I hope?'

How long do we have to wait before it is all right to catch up and have colour? Perhaps when the pagans have got well into videos?

I remember when it was customary to casually place your hand on top of the TV set when entering a room, to see if it was still warm.

Then you knew whether or not it had been suddenly turned off upon your arrival.

A favourite one-liner was: 'We only have it for the news!'

Secret Drinking

It was a very hot sticky day in Northern Minnesota where two of us from England had just finished our ministry at a Camp Meeting. We were glad to be leaving the lakeside camp and the hordes of biting midges. Along with our generous host and his wife we were soon back in their home town and headed for a local restaurant for lunch.

'What'll you drink, Maurice?' enquired our American friend.

'A nice cold beer!' I replied with enthusiasm, knowing we had imbibed together on a previous occasion.

A look of alarm spread over his face as he slowly rose to his feet and, in a kind of semi-crouch, began to peer around the restaurant.

'What on earth are you doing, dear?' enquired his wide-eyed wife.

'Just looking to see if anyone we know is in here!' he whispered back, 'We don't want to cause anyone to stumble.'

'Don't be absurd, dear, I am sure Maurice's beer is not going to offend anyone. After all, you don't have to have one.'

'Please,' I interjected amid the confusion, 'don't bother about me, I'll have a soft drink . . .'

'No, no . . . you have what you want,' the host minister replied with a total lack of conviction and still peering about behind the pillars.

'No use arguing,' I thought.

My associate and I received our cold beers, both with that enticing condensation glistening on the tall glasses; but somehow the edge was taken off the enjoyment. We all felt rather edgy throughout the meal.

Cheers!

A Leadership Lunch

*I*t was many years ago that I was fortunate enough to have lunch sitting alongside the famous 'Galloping Gourmet' of TV fame. True, we were in the company of half-a-dozen other 'national-leaders-types', but I was next to *him*.

I have always been at my most insecure in restaurants. Probably having been bought up in a poor London family, where we used a newspaper for a tablecloth, did not help. Graham was most friendly and unassuming, but his presence caused my insecurities to surface to an alarming level. It was just that everyone made such a fuss of him; folk were coming to our table asking for his autograph, and finally the waiter looked most impressed when The Gourmet Himself smelled the cork and declared the wine was 'perfectly all right'.

By now I was way out of my depth and having trouble making my choice from a simple menu. What I really wanted was the gammon, but I don't like pineapple with it. At home I would have had an egg on top. However that was not an option here, in fact in those far-off days I had never seen what is now on common offer.

Too nervous to discuss the matter in public I ordered the fish!

'And what about you, Sir?' to our esteemed guest.

'I'd like the gammon but would you mind putting a fried egg on top instead of the pineapple?' (Did you guess?)

'Of course not, Sir!'

I wanted to say, 'I'll have that too!', but to change now would seem as if I was eating whatever his lordship ate. Instead I quietly sulked away, glancing covetously at the TV Chef's mouthwatering meal whilst trying to hold my end up in a conversation of great national importance.

If only the plebs had known.

Heavenly Hosts and Divine Secrets

*U*nreality has always worried me. Dear God spare us from it.

Why won't we laugh when things are funny? Do you know I once spent a whole hour speaking from Isaiah on the Seraphims . . . and Terrapins. Yes Terrapins! The first spiritual ministry ever on fresh-water tortoises and nobody laughed. Oh they sniggered, but that just left me wondering what was wrong for sixty long minutes until it was all over. Then my friend told me that I kept calling Teraphims 'terrapins'. Well, thanks.

Mind you it wasn't the only touch of unreality in that morning meeting held in a large house in the West Country on a summer morning long ago. While we were deep in worship, eyes closed and arms in the air, the elderly lady of the house had to be removed to hospital. In order to get her to the front door she had to be stretchered right through the room where we were singing. But we didn't stop. The ambulance men were goggle-eyed as they endeavoured to manoeuvre the groaning ancient through a crush of swaying charismatics who could not, or pretended they could not, see. I guess no one knew what to do and it seemed kind of spiritual to let her be taken off in such an atmosphere. A few of us whispered about doing something, but opted for closed eyes and a few more hallelujahs. I must confess I had one eye open.

Of course you can get yourself all worked up if you peek when you shouldn't as a friend of mine in America found out at a leaders' retreat. They were seated in a circle for prayer when he spied someone on the opposite side of the circle whisper to his neighbour, who in turn whispered to the man by his side. This went on round the circle until the man next to my friend leaned towards his ear. What great revelation was he about to hear? What great secret was being passed from man of God to man of God?

'Your flies are undone!' his neighbour whispered.

Wouldn't it have been easier for the man who spotted the dreadful exposure to have quietly walked round without notifying half the room? There must have been some reason why he didn't, but it eludes me. We've always been a strange lot; but then 'the world' has known that for generations.

Sex Pistols

Sublime innocence can play its part too in the humour of the church.

Several years ago a remarkably good singer who at times travelled the same circuit as me, decided he had a calling to leave secular employment and pursue his gospel singing around the country.

Trying to explain this to his doting mother, who was quite ignorant of the spiritual movement with which he was involved, proved nothing less than hilarious.

Eventually as the light began to dawn, she exclaimed in horror: 'You ain't going to be one of them Sex Pistols are you?'

He related the story to me with a smile and added, 'So much for my Christian witness!'

(Is it necessary to tell you that the Pistols were a famous but outrageous pop group at the time?)

The Pig at the Feast

Friends of ours were invited to the wedding of an earnest, sincere and enthusiastically spiritual couple. The betrothed had a background that could be described as comfortably middle-class but they had found their niche in the genuinely classless society of a substantially black 'Fellowship' in downtown Birmingham. The reception was held in a high-grade hotel on the golf course at Sutton Coldfield. It seems the entire fellowship had been invited to the reception.

Our friends were distant acquaintances of the happy newly-weds and were quite content to find themselves placed on the most distant table, which they shared with an older black couple who were quiet and shy; so smartly dressed, they had hands which displayed the signs of many years of hard and heavy toil. With them also sat two white members of the fellowship, one in his forties, with pinstripes and noticeably few teeth, the other in his twenties with long hair and a knobbly cardigan. Our friends, like the bride and groom, could be described as respectably middle-class, young, of married status.

The six nodded politely to one another and waited for the meal to come. No one said much at first, except for Pinstripes that is, who started into a deeply spiritual conversation with what appeared to be his young disciple. In a very loud voice. The others were obviously meant to be impressed by his profound knowledge. Everyone was forced to listen in as his statements became more and more outrageous, strafed with sporadic volleys of totally unrelated and meaningless scriptures.

Then he turned his didactic abilities to the matter of Law and Grace. 'Of course,' he expostulated, 'we spiritual Christians are not under law; as Paul says, "Exhort servants to be obedient to their masters".'

'Eh?' the others thought, looking about them with embarrassment.

'. . . so you see, personally speaking,' the loud PinStripes continued, 'I wouldn't dream of having a television in the house.'

At this point the gentle black labourer looked up from his meal.

'Woi?' he exclaimed in his broad Brummie voice 'What's wrong with television?'

'Well, you know what Colossians 3:25 says,' instructed Pinstripes patronisingly, 'God is no respecter of persons!'

'Eh?' they all thought once more. The absolute *non-sequitur* of this scripture obviously completely baffled our black friend too.

'Look,' went on the Pinstripes, well into his stride now, 'just name one programme that isn't totally corrupt!'

'Well, Oi loike *Songs of Praise* meself,' confessed the innocent ingenuously. 'Ah!' and here Pinstripes wagged his finger triumphantly, 'but which church does it come from? Tell me that!'

At this point our friends—the husband actually—could stand no more and asked the loudmouthed Pinstripes how many churches there were.

Pinstripes parried defensively and came across with, 'Well, Jesus said, "Do not think I will accuse you to the Father, there is one that accuses you, even Moses in whom ye trust"! '

Husband: 'Isn't there just one Church for whom Christ died and which He loved?' himself by now quoting from the Book of Ephesians. Not one to give up easily he persisted by asking the man why he thought it was that so-called 'Christians' were so exclusive and intolerant of one another.

The Suit was not at all intolerant, he insisted. If only everyone would agree with him, he would tolerate every person in the world!

By now our friends were visibly open-mouthed, but getting tacit support in the form of smiles and twinkle-eyed glances from the Brummie couple.

Suit and his apprentice Cardigan continued with their wild statements, each supported by a stream of quite irrelevant random scriptures. Our storytellers reminded themselves that they were guests at someone else's wedding or they would probably have been very tempted to leave. It proved unnecessary as they were all rescued by the speeches.

As the reception proceedings came to an end, folk broke up into groups and began to drift off. Cardigan approached the husband who had crossed swords with his mentor. 'While the speeches were on,' he confided, 'the Lord told me not to continue the discussion with you. He told me I should not cast pearls before swine.'

Fortunately the couple were both able to laugh, before the husband eyeballed the imaginative disciple and demanded firmly, 'So are you calling me a swine?'

The decidedly unfortunate apprentice shuffled uneasily before continuing, 'Well, er, the Lord told me that. He said I should not talk to you any more.'

'Fine,' responded our irate friend, 'So why are you then?'

'Oh well, I just thought I should tell you what the Lord was saying.'

Meanwhile Pinstripes had approached the lady in the partnership. 'And what were your names again?' he enquired.

'Why? What do you want to know for?' she retorted.

'So that I can remember you,' he intoned with a heavy attempt at spirituality. Presumably he meant 'in prayer'.

'Don't worry,' she replied, 'I don't think you're likely to forget!'

Ask, and Ye Shall Be Turned Down

Way back in 1966 a student from the Home Counties was enjoying college in London. There she had received the elating experience of knowing right now, for that sweet exquisite moment, the full attention of all heaven's angels was focused exclusively upon her, the one sinner who had repented, and was blinking incredulously in the beatific mellow light that had shined in upon her soul.

Aglow with a new joy, she was pleased when a Billy Graham Crusade came to Earl's Court, London—not that she had ever heard of Billy Graham, but she enthusiastically enjoyed the choir and loved the kindly, warm and gentle sparkle which glowed from Cliff Barrows, the musical director.

Suddenly realising how big this Christian world was, and how much there was to absorb, she eagerly volunteered for counselling classes, thus to learn anything going from these ministers who of course knew so very much more than she, and also, maybe, to know how to lead another soul into that same glorious light. She learned well, fulfilled all the tasks, memorised all the set biblical verses, then finally appeared before the panel of ministers who interviewed all would-be counsellors to see if they would be suitable. She jumped willingly through all their theological hoops, answered their questions and confidently quoted the required scriptures and their references. Then, as is customary on such occasions, the interview concluded with the leading cleric asking, 'Any questions?'

'Oh yes sir, please!' This was more than she had hoped for. She sat forward on her chair. There was so very much to learn in this Christian life, and how she would love to sit at these men's feet all day, just asking them questions. Here were three ordained clergymen all to herself, and inviting questions! How many could she ask? How long could they stay? How far dared she go? Better use this Counselling Thing as a starting point she thought.

'John 1:12 says "But as many as received him, to them gave he power (or the right) to become the sons of God",' she hesitated, but the ministers nodded approvingly. It was one of the set verses after all. She continued, 'It doesn't say that those who received him *became* sons, but that they had the *power* to become sons. So then, what exactly *is* a full son, and how does one use that power and actually become one?'

The three horrified clerics immediately thought that after all this teaching, the wretched girl had no idea how to become a Christian after all, and certainly wasn't one herself. They hastily referred her to her own pastor who they recommended should try again to explain the proper steps to salvation, and maybe process another sausage-machine applicant properly. 'Sorry, no counsellor badge for you, Miss. You really must be fully convinced of your own salvation to take this role.'

'Oh, but I am,' she assured them, cheering up at once, 'It is just that . . . '

'No buts! You were questioning the whole concept of regeneration by faith.'

'Oh no Sir, you see . . . ' But there were other candidates waiting to take the test, and it was clearly time to go.

Why didn't the experts understand? The choir was still fulfilling, Cliff Barrows still exuded a kindness and a joy that encouraged her greatly, for she acknowledged it had to be the Real Thing.

Fortunately our would-be keen counsellor was quickly able to overcome her disappointment, and thankfully she was also able to firmly put behind her this first of many brushes with Christianity's middle management.

Perhaps many do not.

On the Terraces at Roker Park

The same young lady turned down as a counsellor in the previous story ran into more trouble twenty years later when attending Roker Park, Sunderland, for another Billy Graham rally; this time with her husband.

During the intervening decades, through various experiences where integrity could not subject itself to conformity, and after more ham-fisted handling by middle management, they found they were not an official part of any particular church group. However, God was still with them and all was well.

They attended the rally with a friend who was afterwards taken up with her Children's Counselling duties, so they sat down on the terraces to await her return. Not far away sat another couple, somewhat older, and obviously in no hurry to drive home or rejoin a coach party.

As our friend caught the older woman's eye, she smiled and greeted her with warm Christian bonhomie. 'Good evening,' she said, 'what a lovely mild night.' Indeed it was, the couple agreed, and asked how far the travellers had come.

'From Middlesborough.'

'Oh yes and which church do you belong to?' Oh dear, now the trouble was going to start.

'We aren't actually part of any formal church,' our lady offered gently.

'Then why didn't you go forward at the appeal? The Lord does want to save, you know!'

'Er, well . . . we didn't say that we were not Christians . . .'

'Well if you don't go to church, but you are saved, then you must be backslidden . . . you should have gone forward to rededicate yourselves to God!'

The backsliders slid back into chapter and verse mode and secretly began to think about Shadrach and his two mates in 3:16 (Daniel that is!). He had answered Nebuchadnezzar, 'We have no need to answer you in this matter!' but our two apparent rebels politely listened to a lecture on 'Not forsaking the assembling of yourselves together, as the manner of some is', with accusing looks at the appropriate moment.

They sighed, knowing full well that to explain would only lead to more unpleasantness. They'd heard it all before, this judgemental farrago, presumably intended in love of course to woo the wandering souls.

To some people the world contains but three stereotypes: the blind unsaved heathen, the faithfully churchgoing 'saved', with all others presumed to be the dangerously backslidden ('Returning to their own vomit' and doomed to end up 'Seven times worse than before', to throw in a couple of convenient texts to bolster the conviction).

Ah well, such are the rewards for passing a cheery greeting, and wishing folks a pleasant 'Good evening!'

Free? Indeed?

'Fanatics have their dreams where-
with they weave/A paradise for a
sect.'

John Keats

'Fanaticism consists in redoubling
your effort when you have forgotten
your aim.'

George Santayana

A Merry Dance

Right from my teens I had been seeking for truth. Even kissing a girl goodnight underneath the stars I would sometimes be thinking. 'This can't be happening. We can't be here. Where did we come from?' Wearily my finite mind wrestled with infinite problems. I even physically pinched myself at times, when questioning if I was really here. I was a small bear with a very small brain. But I was a seeker.

It was on the North-West Frontier of India that I took confirmation classes from a brigadier. That didn't do the trick. I didn't like the man and failed to complete the course.

Years later, repatriated, married and living in the rolling Cotswolds I was still pursuing my search. This included a one-off visit to the village church. The place was vast and nearly empty, yet the local postmistress came and edged me over, stating this had been her family pew for generations. I left in a hurry, informing the rector that I did not wish to cohabit with his miserable congregation. The distressed man suggested I should try looking up and not looking around when I came to worship.

I was much more at home in the pub listening to the landlord singing 'Bless this house', but the inner yearning continued. One night in the back bar of The Plough

I was attending the village All Blacks Football Club meeting in my capacity as secretary. I was in everything! It transpired that no one would approach the rector for his half-a-guinea subscription as a vice-president. They were all certain he would say he had not seen them in church recently. I agreed to go. In fact I wanted to go.

I collected the cheque, left the house and was halfway down steep stone steps from the porch when the rector suddenly blurted out,

'Is everything all right with your soul, Maurice?'

I was startled by such a question, and I think that was when I experienced my first ever touch of the supernatural. For I swear I opened my mouth to say, 'Yes' and I heard myself say 'No'.

I was quickly invited back inside. Not to the lounge this time, but the study. He obviously meant business.

I heard a familiar story which I had always rejected, but this time I accepted. The time seemed right. Next morning the world appeared a new place and I was radiant. My worries had all disappeared.

I went to work, told everyone (of course!) and came home still radiant. Quick as I could I bolted down my dinner and rushed to the rectory to tell the good man that his message had worked. He was out!

Still full of enthusiasm I dashed round the village to an ex-army major with whom I was acquainted.

'I've been converted!' I blurted. No one so fervent as a convert.

The major was stunned. 'Sit down and have a gin and tonic!' he offered.

He seemed to think there was something seriously wrong with me. I said I needed to see the rector and he replied that I needed to see someone! He thought I might find 'the good shepherd' at the village hall where he was due to hand out the spot-prizes at the weekly dance.

Still effervescing, I rushed to the hall and encountered the rector just inside the door looking as if he would rather be anywhere else on earth.

One glance at my changed countenance told its own story and he congratulated me before I said a word. He then said God had told him years ago that one person would be converted under his ministry in the village. I was the one and he was off! He was a Doctor of Divinity, an academic and not suited to parish work, so he said.

I asked where his wife was and he pointed to a spot near the band. I wanted to tell her myself for she had been quite an inspiration to me with her warmth and vivacity.

We were so excited, both being extroverts. We waved our arms in the air and laughed for sheer joy. I felt great, just as though some great river of life was gushing up from inside of me.

As it gushed on I said gallantly, 'May I have this dance?' I'd always been a cool mover!

Her face dropped and she looked suddenly sad.

I wondered what on earth I had said wrong.

'What's the matter?'

Then she gave me my first bit of teaching:

'Christians don't dance, Maurice!'

The first chain was on me and straightaway the honeymoon began to fade.

I knew nothing then of the difference between law and grace.

Lena Zavaroni

For many years I belonged to a segment of evangelical Christianity that believed you never went anywhere without a specific purpose in mind. Especially we did not go where 'unconverted' people were actually enjoying themselves. They were supposed to be madly happy—depending upon what happened to them—whereas we had real joy!

How strange it was not evident.

We had taboos on places and things that circumscribed just about every area the common man had contact with. Pubs and dance halls, theatres and cinemas, alcoholic beverages, cigarettes and TV, make-up and fashion were among the many things we outlawed. My wife and I now call that time our ten lost years; of course it had to be the swinging sixties!

At weddings or similar functions we always left before the action started. At my nephew's wedding breakfast we were nearing the end of the dessert course, when my brother-in-law said with a pleasant touch of sarcasm, 'You'll be off soon then, Maurice?' They knew us too well. I told him that on this occasion we would like to stay. (My wife has never understood why I ever got into all this absurdity anyway, but she dutifully abided by the rules set by the head of the house.)

We sat at a table near the wall of course, and began to pray quietly for God to help us survive in this den of possible iniquity, with its flashing strobe lights and ultraloud music. I thought I heard that familiar small voice inside me whispering, 'Don't tell me lies, Maurice; you love the lights and the noise!'

Yes, I suppose I do really.

Soon a small tubby girl just like my surreptitious TV idol, Lena Zavaroni, came over and started to chat. She spoke endlessly of her cat and her parrot who apparently did not get along too well. No matter to me how small the talk, it was a great help to a stranger in that alien culture.

Eventually her father signalled me over, fetched me a drink and expressed the hope that his daughter was not being too much of a nuisance. Being my usual over-the-top transparent self, I told him she was actually being a help as I was not used to this kind of atmosphere.

He was genuinely inquisitive and questioned me about my abstinence, so I quite naturally explained to him all about my faith in God and the weird paths it had led me into. The man was quite knocked out, in fact said he felt moved and thought he would never be the same again. Then he thanked me profusely for being so open and friendly.

'You ought to frequent these places more,' he said, 'Folk need what you have got!' (Oh, really?)

On returning to my table, I found little Lena had tired of talking and wanted to dance. She could only have been about twelve years old, but she was robust and started to drag me towards the dance floor. Rather than cause a scene I quietly succumbed and eased to the edge where I started to move in time with the rock and roll music.

Before long a shout went up from the centre of the

floor urging me to join in with the main throng. Before long I was exercising with the best of them and thoroughly enjoying myself. Who was it told me Christians shouldn't dance? What nonsense!

After a while a guest about my age left his seat at the edge and joined awkwardly in the action. He leaned toward me and demanded tensely in a strong Scottish accent, 'What age are you?'

'That's it . . .' I thought, 'I have been found out!'

When he discovered I was past fifty, he marvelled to see a middle-aged man enjoying this young style of music so much and observed that I must be a regular dancing man to have kept up with the trends.

Still moving in time with the beat I told him this was a kind of first for me, I had been in the backwoods for years.

'What do you mean?' he enquired shouting above the music.

Punching my fist the air, I called back: 'I am a Christian!'

He was obviously offended. With a superior air he informed me that he was a good Presbyterian and went and sat down again.

I could not see the connection.

Inside a very short time I had obviously been a source of life and hope to one person and the opposite to another. I reasoned that perhaps one was a plain honest man and the other a self-righteous religious person.

However, one thing I knew for sure, this was where I belonged.

With people.

As I sat and sipped and pondered, I remembered Jesus' last recorded petition to His Father before He left this earth: 'I pray that you would not take them out of this world.'

I realised that for over ten years I had cut myself off from many fine ordinary people and all that healthy enjoyment too!

Still I had learned now. Better late than never.

Floridian Mystic

I recommended a book by Matthew Fox to my Michael Spillane (not the Micky Spillane) from West Palm Beach, but he was not able to purchase it at the traditional Christian bookshop. Upon further investigation he was advised to try the New Age bookstore.

He went with considerable trepidation because some years before he had weakly endeavoured to witness to the owner with very little success. The man, originally from the Antipodes, was a well-known local figure who had long hair and wore a hairband. He could often be seen as dawn broke standing on one leg facing eastwards out to sea.

As Mike crept in he was glad to go unrecognised as he stood in line behind an elderly lady who was complaining that her crystal did not work and insisting upon a refund.

Eventually, still thankfully unrecognised, he faced the unusual man eye to eye and was informed that the book was indeed in stock. Moments later he was on the pavement with his purchase thinking to himself . . . I must write to Maurice.

I can still vividly recall his letter to me saying:

'What has happened to me, Maurice, since getting to know you? Here is the once straight laced evangelical standing in line in a New Age bookshop behind an eccentric lady holding up a crystal, remonstrating with a longhaired mystic with a headband who stands on one leg on the seashore at dawn watching the sun rise from the East!'

Still, life has ceased to be boring!

No Smoke Without Fire

It was in the early days of the House Church Movement and many of the 'converts' came from the denominations. If charged with poaching sheep from other folds our normal reply was that we just grew greener grass.

The mid-week guest speaker was an elderly Scot with a laid-back style and an impeccable English accent. He evoked consternation with his very earliest remarks.

'I don't bother much with sin these days,' he began. 'I can't bear to get up in the morning in order to dig a hole and jump in.' His audience began to stir uneasily. 'After all, it's God's job to keep me clean, I certainly cannot manage it myself!'

The religious listeners began to fume as the man from over the border unfolded the freedom in which he walked. The smoke, however, literally began to rise when, at the close of his talk, the speaker lit up a cigarette and asked, 'Any questions?' Strange, isn't it, how talk of liberty is one thing, to practise it, quite another.

Any questions, indeed! 'Licence was what he was into,' they said 'If we were meant to smoke we would have been born with a chimney on our head!' As for sin, it appeared that every night before going to bed they knelt down and asked forgiveness for all the sins they had committed during the day. On awaking next morning they began it all again. What they had been up to in the night I could not imagine.

The speaker, though, commendably felt only sympathy for his hearers.

'Oh dear,' he said with unfeigned concern. 'It must be a miserable existence!'

And that night changed my whole life.

Strong Medicine

I am constantly amazed at how we tend to mistake national religious customs for spirituality, yet when viewed globally they are all very different. A little travel broadens the mind.

For instance in Argentina, they wouldn't undress to swim, nor must they whistle. In Hungary they smoked freely; American women wore make-up but wouldn't drink, the Germans drank beer but banned make-up (or make believe as it was called); whilst in Britain we eschewed smoking, drinking, cosmetics and dancing although we were allowed whistling and swimming, except of course on Sundays!

On the Isle of Thanet in Kent refusal to touch alcohol on religious grounds was taken to extremes. The Pauline injunction to 'take a little wine for your stomach's sake' was the cue for zealous intercessors to accompany their petitions with a gentle rubbing of wine into the patient's stomach—always seemed a little kinky to me!

Travelling down the Rhine one time, 'ministering' to groups here and there, my companion and I were offered wine with our meal served in very large tumblers. We both accepted, just to be sociable, even though my friend had never tasted alcohol before. The conversation flowed, through an interpreter of course, and as the meal progressed I was offered, and accepted, another tumbler of wine. Our host then turned to my friend and said, 'More wine, Herr . . ?'

I suddenly became acutely aware of his unusually rosy cherubic face and brightly shining eyes and, as if in a dream, heard him reply,

'Yyesh pleash!'

It was undoubtedly a conversion experience and his heart had been made very glad!

Need a Repray?

Whilst many of us, from outside, complained bitterly about Anglican liturgy, the extemporary prayer of which we were so proud was oft times couched in archaic third-rate language, full of clichés.

At the prayer meeting there was always one supermarket intercessor who filled the prayer basket with every conceivable topic from Mrs Jones' gout to all the mission fields in Africa, along with 'all those laid aside everywhere'! What dread euphemisms were used for being ill. What laughable (had we dared) gaffes sometimes ensued.

For instance, I am sure that this old chestnut must be rooted in fact: 'Dear Father, thou knowest that dear brother Bill is lying at death's door, wilt thou please hasten to pull him through.'!

Indeed, I actually heard a prayer during a packed service of celebration held in Goodmayes, East London, which ran: 'Lord, we pray for our sister, Mrs X, who is laid on one side in a bed of sickness . . . do undertake for her, dear Lord.'

I was left with a deluge of questions. What is the matter with her other side? Did God mercifully remove our 'sister' to the local funeral parlour? And just what is a bed of sickness . . . ugh!

I've always maintained the Christian faith is a mystery.

Comic Opera

Perhaps the most unbelievable and outrageous meeting I attended was in a town in the Yorkshire Dales. It was my first visit and, accompanied by a young singer-guitarist, I sat waiting for the proceedings to begin.

For years the growing number of people I associated with—later to be known as the House Church Movement—had been obsessed with a line of teaching known as 'Body Ministry'. Implicit within this teaching was the fact that everyone should participate in the meetings, not just the leaders. Of course, under this covering brief all sorts of weird and wonderful things could take place, as the carnal desire to be noticed, or to be important, encouraged the unaccomplished to head for the spiritual limelight.

Soon after the music began, a demure lady of advancing years, overdressed in somewhat old-fashioned clothing, made for the centre of the room and began an eccentric slow solo dance. I whispered to the main leader that she seemed rather an unusual type of person for our meetings. 'Used to be an opera singer,' he confided in a low voice, as though that explained everything.

My eyes had also settled on a middle-aged man sitting opposite me who appeared to be wearing a home-made ginger-coloured bird's nest which had dropped askew onto his head. He was tall and gaunt with an extremely sad face. To my amazement he left his seat and began a very exaggerated form of Latin dance around the swaying lady pensioner.

They held each other's eyes in rapt attention and I

felt for a moment that I could be watching some ancient mating rite. At this point I also noticed that everyone had 'gone spiritual' and closed their eyes. I can't say I blamed them. The whole scene was most embarrassing.

I turned to my young friend to assess his reaction, for in these situations of group pressure it is easy to start believing that you are the one who is cuckoo, as everyone else is accepting what is happening. Unfortunately he could not whisper to me his opinion as he had his handkerchief stuffed in his mouth to prevent him breaking into uncontrollable laughter.

That did it. For the rest of the meeting we were like two naughty children who dare not even glance at each other for fear of getting out of control.

Later that day I openly approached the overall leader of the group. 'Can't you do anything about those dancers? If anyone comes in from outside they will think we are all completely off our heads.' He began to make excuses for them by saying they both had very sad lives. I sympathised, but said I felt there should be a better way of finding solace other than inflicting this performance on the whole congregation week by week.

As I pursued the matter I also learned that the man was receiving financial support from the group as he was hard-up. He had been approached many times about the dancing and asked not to participate unless he felt clearly motivated to do so, but apparently he regularly received strong 'leadings'.

'Can't you tell him not to dance?' I pleaded. 'It can't go on.' 'Oh, it is no use telling him, I am afraid,' the leader explained. 'You see, he has a will of iron!'

I never heard what became of the lady opera singer,

but sadly I did hear that the man with the thatch died a sudden early death. On my next visit I made enquiries.

'Do you know,' said one of the group members, 'it turned out he had lots of money after all . . . and he left it to an Animal Sanctuary!'

'Pity he never brought some of the animals to the meetings!' I responded with irritation. 'We had everything else happening.'

My sadness at our lamentable discernment and ineffectiveness deepened, and I began to wonder more and more if we were perhaps missing the way. It was a good many years before the absurdity of our meeting-orientated lifestyle fully dawned on me. But I am glad it did.

Driven Potty

That everyone in community doesn't see eye to eye seems well established fact, but most neighbours managed to live together in a substantial measure of harmony. years ago—before present-day insularity and the ghastly concept of 'nuclear families' was common.

Decades ago now and greatly flushed with charismatic enthusiasm, some of us designed to go much further. Following hard upon the heels of our biblical forerunners—depicted in the Acts of the Apostles as 'having all things in common'—we moved into a large Dower House on the Essex–London border. It was a grand mansion indeed, but sadly in need of repair, and I remember harbouring morbid fears that it would all end up looking dreadfully tatty, the kind of 'Christian effort' I had witnessed so often in the old houses of Olde England. With the constant lack of funds I felt we would inevitably install furniture that was by no means commensurate with the majestic grandeur of the property. In this respect, among others, along with the longsuffering Job 'All that I feared came upon me' as I tried to learn to live with dreary incongruity.

The two pioneer families moved in first and intended to develop slowly, but before you could say 'Judas Iscariot' we had thirty-six men, women and children all bedded down under one roof. Just how it happened I will never know. As usual I was equipped with my fine pair of rose-coloured spectacles and expected us all to flow together in 'wonder, love and praise', to quote the inspired hymnwriter. Well, it didn't quite work out like that, I can assure you.

Just for starters let me inform you that until then I had imagined everyone lived their lives by and large along the same guidelines by which my wife and I had successfully charted ours for so many years. Now that was definitely a mistake.

Just to isolate but one instance, and to be absolutely mundane, let me confess that I hardly knew the purpose of a child's potty. Seldom, if ever, had I witnessed the receptacle in use, and certainly I had never, but never, administered the same, whether in times of normality or even dire need. We had distinct parent roles as you can see.

The first new family to move in I had known for years. They were always so easy to get along with—that is, until the very first morning when they made their appearance around the large communal fireplace in the main entrance hall. To my utter amazement they boldly carried in this most obnoxious (I very nearly said 'odious') of objects, then stripped their youngest infant down to the skin and enthroned him in full view. Drying nappies were soon flapping a welcome from the radiators, just inside the double entrance doors. Frankly, I was speechless.

Right there and then, I guess, the silent inner roots of bitterness began to spring up inside me and no doubt they defiled many, as so aptly predicted by the writer to the Hebrews.

Furthermore, we had always been used to an orderly meal table. 'Seen and not heard' was definitely our motto for the children. At this board I could not be heard myself. Our children generally ate what was placed in front of them without complaint, except of course in the eyes, whereas others, to my amazement, made short work of informing everyone in a bellowing voice that the food was horrid and they were not going to eat it.

Oh, the times I longed to put my foot on some dear little chest and shovel the food in! Instead I regularly retired to our one quiet room, for all the children slept dormitory-style way above, fell on my knees and groaned out my complaints to heaven.

It was a crash course in sanctification, for others as well as me no doubt; for by no means am I inferring that my way was the right way. In fact I now know it was very far from perfect, and if I had my time again there would be very little that I would repeat. I just didn't understand kids or teenagers. It was a different way, that is for sure.

We lasted for just two years and I am sure others were as pleased to see us go as we were to leave. It says something I suppose that we are still friends today, but not close friends, mind you!

I discovered, yet again the hard way, that we were never meant to copy the New Testament history. Looking back I still feel I really did hear that Inner Voice whispering, 'The church is a community, Maurice'; but I guess I rushed off without waiting to hear more. In what way was it a community? Whilst the quiet voice was whispering 'A', I had quickly added 'B, C, D, E' and dashed off in typical fashion to produce another abortive fiasco. I have never been a sluggard!

It was all very painful and I really hope some of it was worthwhile and that I learned some valuable lessons, but offhand I cannot think what they were!

Given the Runaround

There was a time when demon activity was blamed for every problem in the church and these little devils were seen lurking behind every curtain.

With some trepidation an acquaintance of mine took a friend for his first visit to a Charismatic meeting. They entered rather late and the singing was already in progress. As the congregation sang lustily, the exuberant minister was shouting 'Praise the Lord!' and 'Hallelujah!' whilst running on the spot in time with the music.

The couple were creeping surreptitiously down a side aisle, when the extrovert on the platform thrust out a pointing finger in the direction of the first-timer and declared in a loud voice that he had a demon.

This exuberant leader shouted over the music. He said that if the possessed individual would start to run round the church everyone else would continue to praise the Lord and then the demon would be exorcised. The man would then experience his deliverance and be set free.

The more experienced of the two took his seat, looking agog as his guest began hesitantly to run down one aisle and up the other.

Round and round he went, gaining speed as the praise rose higher and higher.

At the crescendo the minister screamed in a mighty voice, 'You're free! You're free!'

He then encouraged the tiring visitor to return to his seat.

Once there, with the voluminous singing still in full

spate, the poor man sat looking bewildered and disorientated.

His concerned host whispered to him above the din, 'You don't have a demon, do you?'

The man replied that he did not think so.

'Well, why on earth did you run round like that then?'

Spreading both hands in a gesture of despair, the newcomer said weakly, 'Well, what can you do?'

What indeed?

Bring a Bucket

Across the country the obsession with demonic activity reached such alarming proportions that it was dangerous to cough in some meetings lest someone bellowed out triumphantly, 'There goes another one!'

Meanwhile down in Somerset it was well known that buckets were readily on hand for folk to retch into whilst their deliverance was being administered. Such unhealthy occupation lead many to spend half the night 'delivering' others from dozens of demons, but unfortunately this left the person being set free in no better condition the next morning.

Then came the phase where the person in trouble was required to name the unholy resident, or rather the demon itself was to speak. Someone close to me admitted that in the middle of the long night he told the ministering couple, 'I am beginning to make them up now!'

All this was not done without sincerity, but we have to conclude that it was mostly sincerely wrong.

Of course, there were genuine cases of folk being helped, but these were occasional and vastly outnumbered by those where young people were confused or even, in a few cases, permanently damaged. Many willingly took on the role of amateur psychiatrists and others became pale imitations of New Testament exorcists.

The writer personally knows of one couple in Hertfordshire who baptised their cat to set it free, and also sawed the top off their wardrobe because of the influence it was supposed to be having on the household. Getting into such realms of fantasy inevitably led some couples into sexual fantasies too, and eventually sexual exploits best left untold.

How low can we sink in the name of the work of God? The pain inflicted can make one very angry if you dwell upon it. Still I guess, as one well-known expositor among us used to say, 'Deception is deception! It is no use being annoyed with a blind man if he bumps into you in the street. His problem is he cannot see.'

Pondering that can give one a devil of a headache.

Roadie

Public meetings always conceal a great element of risk, but I am adamant that the premium on Christian efforts should be loaded.

The fiasco in Chadwell Heath, east of London, I remember all too well. There I stood at the head of the chancel steps in full flow, but having a little trouble with the microphone (which is quite normal by the way). We were living OK with the whistling feedback, but this was followed by intermittent breaks in transmission, so that one moment I was whispering and the next bellowing, as I raised my voice to compensate. I seemed especially gifted at raising my voice the precise moment the sound returned. The message was definitely beginning to lose impact.

Nigel was a charming fellow and ever ready to assist. We should have refused his help and looked for someone else, but he had such a big heart—I told you it was a Christian effort! As I struggled on I caught sight of him on full hands and knees advancing down the centre aisle, trying to trace the fault. Of course every time he rattled the wires the speakers erupted with a loud burp.

Trying to be surreptitious, he was all the more conspicuous. Whilst every ear was trying to concentrate on my important message, every eye was straying to the centre aisle and I could see some folk actually nudging their neighbours to make sure they did not miss the action.

Nearer and nearer the front he advanced, seemingly oblivious to the great distraction being caused. He crossed the no-man's land between the front pew and the steps still on all fours, and still devoutly tracing the wires in front of him with all the patience of a sapper in a live minefield.

When he finally advanced up the three steps and headed for the microphone, I really should have stopped the proceedings there and then, but somehow I missed my opportunity and decided to keep on going.

When he actually brushed my trouserlegs I had to look down to see what was happening. I was standing astride the cable and realised to my horror that he was attempting the impossible, which was to get through my legs and trace the fault as he went.

I struggled to keep my balance as I stood on tiptoe, continuing to speak through the crackling transmission whilst by now astride Nigel's back.

Well, he did get through! But someone laughed and released pandemonium.

Eventually even the platform party joined in, and I just hope the poor man did not get too hurt by the hilarity at his expense. I don't think he did, for he continued right on tracing without even an upward glance.

Does this sort of thing happen to ordinary mortals or only to those who are trying so hard to convince the world of their contact with the Source of All Power?

Satanic Attack

Conferences were always felt to be the highlight of our year in the denomination without a name to which I used to belong. The annual conferences were held at 'The Centre' in South London. The suburb was named Honor Oak and—avoiding a name (or 'nomen') at all costs—the centre was referred to by many in hushed tones as H. O. I thought it meant Head Office for years! Here resided The Leaders who were the custodians of the greater revelations which our people understood and others did not.

After one excellent oration I commented to a very spiritual-looking lady that I thought the ministry was very good.

'Good? Good?' she exclaimed with dismay, and pointed to the skies 'It was up there! Up there!'

Well, I could not go that far.

I soon realised that there were a host of elderly spinsters who hung upon every word that the aristocratic leader uttered. He gave us the feeling that we were the pioneers and 'pressing through' against great odds. Perhaps he did not know that the first will be last?

This deception of our superiority was exposed to me when a charming, but very intense elderly lady explained what a battle it had been and what suffering she had experienced, in order to get to the conference that day and hear the message of the hour. She said that 'The Devil' had been attacking her all morning in an attempt to prevent her attendance.

I was obviously alarmed and enquired, 'What do you mean, he attacked you?'

'That's it precisely!' she replied with extreme gravity, 'First thing this morning the milkman came extra early and made such a rattle with the bottles that I lost an hour of sleep. I need to be fresh to take in all the Lord has to say.'

Now I was getting confused.

'Then while I was making breakfast the milk boiled over, causing me a great delay.'

'Really?' I ventured.

'Finally as I was approaching The Centre, my suspender broke and my stocking started to slide down my leg. It was awful. I commanded at once, "Get behind me, Satan!"'

She was deadly serious. I had to turn my head and permit myself a sly smile at the thought of the devil grappling with this elderly lady's leg in order to prevent her spiritual progress.

I felt a little sad too. Sorry for her in her delusion, and also for all those folk (some who called themselves Christian and others who did not) who were truly suffering that morning—maybe lying in the local hospital beds unable to make a conference meeting even if they wanted to.

As we all know, there is a lot of pain in the world.

However, I still permitted myself the luxury of that smile.

Chinese Confusion

Pronunciation has always been a weakness of mine and often makes me the butt of family humour.

Before introducing an oriental young man to the Sunday morning meeting I asked his name. After several pathetic attempts to get it right he suggested I just use his forename . . . 'Foo'. Many did, he said.

I stood and made a formal introduction, giving a little of his history and his successes. Foo was now a senior surgeon in Los Angeles. Foo, in spite of his extreme youth, was now designing equipment for complicated operations. The great Foo was this and the great Foo was that.

Every time I mentioned his name he smiled broadly and finally began to laugh audibly. I asked what was so humorous and he stood to explain to everyone.

'We use the same word for several different meanings. We differentiate by pronouncing the words in different ways. I tried to convey the right sound to Maurice, but he is actually calling me . . . "Mr Trousers".'

I am sure with a little more practice we could have got this right before the meeting. I think it was possibly his party piece!

The Bishop's Trousers

Truthfulness is undoubtedly of the essence, but not of course so as to unnecessarily offend. The first question I ever asked a clergyman in my early conversion years was, 'Why have you got your collar on back to front?' Not exactly the best way to win friends and influence people.

Meanwhile my dedication to absolute honesty meant I spent years putting in hours of overtime I did not get paid for, but would not have dreamed of bringing home a paper clip that did not belong to me. That would have been stealing, I reasoned. The Book of Proverbs calls it being 'righteous overmuch' I believe.

Certainly my attitude did not endear me to many people. I told them I was holy and in no uncertain terms.

I have learned the hard way that there is a place for kindness and tact even in correction, but I still find it very difficult to dissemble in any form. Yet I do know there is no need to go around hurting everyone.

I am reminded of an aged tailor I knew who told me of a rotund bishop in the Midlands for whom he had produced a pair of bespoke trousers. After a few days he returned to enquire if they were entirely satisfactory.

The wise bishop first informed him that when he was walking about they were perfectly comfortable. So far so good. 'However . . .' he continued in a soft voice as he then crouched down and produced a most pained expression on his face whilst sighing, ' . . . But when I sit down . . . oh oh oooh!!'

Neither seat nor crutch had actually ripped, but the truthful message of severe constriction was delicately conveyed.

Masterly.

A Sizeable Churchgoer

Soon after my entry into the ranks of Evangelical Christianity I was cajoled into door-to-door evangelism.

I even talked my wife into it and she absolutely hated the job. Well, to be truthful, her efforts were limited to popping *Challenge* newspapers through letterboxes. I shall never forget the sight of her creeping up those paths making as little sound as possible, taking ages to silently insert the *Good Newspaper* into each letterbox lest she disturb someone within and be cornered into conversation. Eileen is more of a 'sweet savour' of God than a mouthpiece; but we would not settle for that.

You hear some funny things on doorsteps from people who are embarrassed and really want shot of you. Once in the mining village of Aylesham in Kent we were dutifully endeavouring to recruit the unchurched to attend a rally in the Baptist Church. We were not getting much of a response but were collecting a bevvy of imaginative excuses.

The cake goes to a rotund middle-aged miner's wife who declared with absolute resoluteness: 'No thanks dearie, I am all right. You see, my mother was a Big Baptist!'

Thankfully Roy, the erstwhile evangelist, successfully kicked the temptation to counter, 'I bet she was!'

I hope my doorstep responses to the Jehovah's Witnesses and the Mormons have a little more inspiration. But somehow I think there is a great similarity between their efforts and mine. We all managed to convey that for us 'all the answers were in' (to quote a good friend of mine) but now I go through life with a lot less dogmatism and a lot more mystery, and I hope a greater attraction than in my know-it-all days.

I know Eileen is pleased to be off the treadmill.

Digest the Message

Many know that the prophet Ezekiel was commanded to eat a scroll, but few know of a modern sequel. My information is second-hand, but even allowing for discrepancies in transmission, it is worthy of a mention.

We go back to the days when we were all intrepid Bible smugglers following in the path of the renowned Brother Andrew. Slipping through the Iron Curtain with a stashed car was a must for a Charismatic medal ribbon. Looking back it does seem many of us had boarded the bandwaggon of the latest Christian in-thing. With our bumbling subterfuge it is a wonder we did not get many local believers locked up for years. Best not to dwell upon that thought too long!

On the inauspicious occasion in question trouble began within a mile or two of Calais. Being asked whether he had decided to go into Poland or Romania first, the hesitant leader informed the driver that he was not sure yet. His guidance was apparently slow in coming through and his forward planning was legend.

'You'd better decide soon,' replied the driver. 'I have to turn left or go straight on in a minute!'

No decision was made so they went straight on. Yugoslavia was always a doddle—no trouble until you tried to leave and penetrate further into Eastern Europe. This was not the case for the fated agent 'X' who was followed the moment he crossed into President Tito's domain. The target man was a prominent Christian in Romania. The contraband was in the form of some eagerly awaited letters and a message on tape from a fellow countryman presently on the staff at Oxford University.

The driver of X's vehicle related to me how difficult things became once they crossed the Romanian border. The road signs were impossible and communicating with nationals without knowledge of their language equally so. This was highlighted upon their first attempt to find a caravan park. Being totally lost in a grey city centre the group leader was forced to disembark and make enquiries. He chose an elderly inoffensive woman on a street corner and shouted in a guttural voice, 'Camp! Camp!' The poor soul was frightened out of her life and started to scream.

The commotion brought soldiers running to her aid with bayonets fixed, as our heroes drove off at top speed. It was soon evident they were being closely followed by an armed policeman on a motorcycle. Nevertheless they were forced to stop and ask again and again, each time producing the inevitable, 'Camp! Camp!'

Finally someone showed recognition, pointed straight out of town and also managed to indicate that it was several miles away. The terrain became bleak and desolate as they drove further and further east. The only person seen on the entire journey since leaving the city was the motorcyclist riveted in their rear mirror.

The infiltrators were almost at the point of despair when hope dawned in the form of an immense encampment which loomed out of the now-darkening sky. As they approached the enormous gates the sentries gave away the secret—it was an army camp, not a caravan camp they had been directed to. I would love to have personally observed that abrupt U-turn.

The decision was made on the move; they would quit the country with the mission unaccomplished. Cut their losses. It was evident that to seek out the underground Christian whilst they had a motorcycle escort was inviting trouble. All the way to the border the policeman stuck closer than a brother, only pausing to use his radio link.

Now they had to face the problem of getting the letters and the tape out of the country! Pulling into a layby just short of the border, they were forced to make the biggest decision of the trip: they would eat their sandwiches in full view of the patrol and secretly consume the letters between the slices. (This was real international espionage stuff, without the rice paper.)

As the leader himself steadfastly devoured the written words, the problem of the tapes presented itself. I would be delighted to relate how inch by inch they were threaded down his gullet on the blind side of the state police; but my licence does not extend that far. To the best of my knowledge they were forced to risk smuggling them out again, without even spending a night in enemy territory.

What I do know is that a final decision was made not to waste the trip, but to finish off with a holiday in Venice. Well, that was sensible, wasn't it?

I never thought to ask about Poland.

Perhaps it was just as well.

End-Time Revelation?

Have you ever participated in that quiet singing that emanates from any group of people sitting with their eyes closed, heaving deep sighs of spiritual contentment, having completely lost touch with their minds? Well, to such a company anything is possible, indeed quite probable.

Perhaps the nicest story from such an environment was enacted in a public meeting in Surrey. The silence was long and pregnant, the atmosphere charged with 'oohs' and 'aahs', when a sweet soft voice of a swaying worshipper intoned the words of a familiar chorus, having, it appears, inadvertently changed the gender:

> 'He'll be coming round the mountain when
>   he comes,
> He'll be coming round the mountain when
>   he comes,
> He'll be coming round the mountain,
> Coming round the mountain . . .'

Soon most of the room was crooning vacantly along, unaware of the slip that had been made.

I'd like to say that it was when they reached the line, 'He'll be wearing pink pyjamas', that the penny dropped, but honesty forbids. In fact, this is a case where I was not there at all, but I do have the story on reliable authority.

I bet there were some red faces about, unless of course someone tried to pretend that God was leading them into the song after all. From past experience I would say it was a dead cert no one laughed, but rather tried to find some serious way out of the dilemma.

I am not at all sure just how 'He will be coming', but I am full of expectancy. Somehow I don't think it will be round the mountain.

Carried Away

Since writing earlier about the lady who was stretchered out through a meeting in Taunton I have met up again with Dave, the singer who was with me on this occasion. He reminded me how, whilst the lady was resting in another room awaiting an ambulance to take her to hospital, he and I tried to keep the meeting going.

Although remembering our embarrassment at the time, I had quite forgotten the punchline.

'Play something Dave,' I said when she finally emerged prostrate on the stretcher. Everyone had their eyes closed, mumbling under their breath and pretending the scene was not happening. Apparently I wanted to help the atmosphere along, thinking also the lady would enjoy the music to encourage her on her way.

'Jesus Take Me As I Am,' he struck up.

What else?

'Another fine mess you've gotten us into.'

The Assembling of Yourselves

'The thought came to me that little boys play with wooden swords and will be soldiers when they grow up, and little girls play with dolls and will be mothers tomorrow. And we humans cherish certain images and with them play at religion but when we have grown, what shall we become?'

Lanza del Vasto

'I have come that you might have meetings and have them more abundantly.'

Anon.

The Ministers' Fraternal

The onslaught began the moment I put my head through the door.

It was already with some trepidation that as a novice from the newly formed House Church Movement, I attempted to hob-nob with the ministers of the established churches in the town. But this I had not expected.

'Ah, The House Church man! What's this we hear about lots of people all living together in one household?'

'Yes, single girls giving all their money to the head of the house and then doing whatever he wants?'

'Sounds like the natural breeding ground for immorality, which we have heard is happening in some of your groups.'

My rather feeble interjections of 'Pardon . . . well . . . but . . .' did nothing to stem the flood of protestation and just as I was thinking that retreat was my only form of possible defence, the benign Catholic priest came to my rescue. One of 'these girls', he said generously, was working in his school and she was just about the best teacher that he had ever encountered.

'Actually, she lives in my house,' I gasped with some relief and headed for a chair in the corner where I tried to blend with the wallpaper.

Tea and biscuits over, I began to realise that the main item on the monthly agenda was fixing the date of the next meeting, and I had obviously been a welcome diversion. However, on this occasion there was another topic: the proposed Annual Service of Unity to be staged on a nearby village green. We drew out our diaries and flipped endlessly, but no unity could be found as to a common date.

The irascible Baptist minister began to mutter that if the Catholics did not observe so many unbiblical feast days then these yearly meetings of witness would be easier to fix. I sensed the chill wind of division begin to blow through the manse. The priest, in spite of being the apparent cause of the current difficulty, was quite the most reasonable of men. Why didn't we just go ahead without him, he suggested, as we all seemed in so much more of a hurry?

The rather meek Methodist took this as his cue to gently enquire how long the Father actually thought it would be before all barriers were down and we could regularly worship together as one congregation.

After very evident deliberation came the Father's slow sincere answer: 'Oh . . . I should think about . . . five hundred years . . .'

'Five hundred years!' the Baptist again, and seriously annoyed.

After more discussion, the amiable Father eventually succumbed to peer pressure and agreed that his people should participate on one of their feast days. He would encourage them to come, he said, but he would not be answerable as to their condition.

'Whatever do you mean?' shouted the staunch upholder of total immersion in nothing but H_2O, who was by now dangerously red in the face and obviously very angry.

The priest, still the tranquil epitome of toleration, informed us all without concern that his people loved to celebrate on such occasions and so they might well be slightly inebriated.

'Do you mean . . . d-d-drunk?' came the near-apoplectic reply from the Reverend You-Know-Who.

After that it was all downhill. The meeting degenerated into a frosty shambles, with all notion of possible unity well and truly gone.

The discussion concerning the service-on-the-green was delicately postponed until the following month, but needless to say, I was not there to participate. I had better things to do.

Since then I have realised that unity cannot be arranged from the top, for so many church leaders are defensive and perhaps just a little afraid of the disintegration of their own smaller empires of influence. In fact, if it were not for the leaders with their different emphases, maybe God's people might just be one anyway. Well, it's a thought!

Alas, soon afterwards the unfortunate Baptist minister died of a heart attack; but the Roman father is, I believe, still alive and celebrating.

Charismatic Rave-Up

Just think of it: thirty years of meetings, and several in a week for many of those years, since my first conscious encounter with God. That is a large slice of my life. Instead of realising that it was in fact *Life* that my rescuer was offering so freely, somewhere along the line I was sold a mickey and ended up believing.

'I have come that you might have meetings and have them more abundantly.'

And how varied those meetings were! From the sober beginnings in a Cotswold Anglican Church where we sat fifteen feet apart and hardly acknowledged each other's presence, to the ultimate Charismatic rave-ups in that grand ballroom over the Cauliflower Public House in Ilford, east of London, where we danced the hours away. Those were remarkable days no doubt. I once remember the publican standing outside the open door holding the telephone aloft towards our meeting upstairs:

'It's them upstairs, dear,' he said, returning the instrument to the speaking position. 'They are having a better time up there than the customers down in the bar.' We were too!

It was in Fort Lauderdale, Florida, where I swung the microphone on the end of a lead and lifted the elegant congregation of five hundred to such dizzy heights in a swinging little number called 'City of God'. As I floated upon a wave of elation back towards my seat, I was clasped in a firm embrace by a most attractive elderly lady with a wide-brimmed hat and a smile to match. She looked for all the world as if she kept Christian Dior in business single-handed.

'You are the greatest thing to hit America since Rudi Valee,' (in the twenties?) she purred in my ear as I sought to unravel myself.

It was certainly a far cry from the severe restraint of the village church where I first realised my need of some divine assistance to make it through the striving Vanity Fair of the fifties.

Yes, we had come a long way too since my early immediately post-Anglican days when I used to watch from an upstairs window as the 'Company' (a term lifted from the Acts of the Apostles, by the way) cheerfully came to meet in a back street in Canterbury city. In those days I observed them lose all semblance of joy once on the premises. Religion was a serious business. They had come to *sing* about joy, not *be* joyful.

Comings and Goings

How well I remember that small sincere group in Canterbury that used to meet under the joint leadership of a few of us 'elders' (each in our late twenties or early thirties). It was all so soon after my initial revelation of the Almighty and I was far too keen and radical for the orthodox folds to contain me. 'No one so zealous as a convert,' it is truthfully said.

We clung together as the 'only true church' for well over ten years. Near the end of my tenure we invited a gifted, hale and hearty man from Somerset to visit us. He was a powerful preacher, we had heard. As we embarked upon our opening extempore prayers the poor man became openly perplexed.

'As we come into your presence today, dear Lord . . .' we began, following hard one upon another. Finally he could bear it no longer, stood to his feet and blurted out, 'Where have you all been then?'

He took the opportunity at this early juncture to 'minister the word', as we called preaching the sermon in those days. At very great length he informed us that God was always with us and in us. We didn't have to go anywhere to find Him, or bring Him down. It was heady stuff.

After he had finished we completed our unwritten liturgy by singing another hymn and bowing our heads for the final prayers.

'As we leave your presence, dear Lord . . .' began one after another.

'Where are you all going now?' demanded our speaker, who evidently felt he had wasted his journey and his breath.

Well, maybe not. Perhaps some seeds were sown that were to bear fruit many years later. How an honourable pursuit after godliness led to such a boring and debilitating disease as meetingitis I do not know . . . But sufficient to say I have been cured!

The West Country preacher, who has now finished his earthly pilgrimage, could be another of those smiling down on me right now. I have heard him at last, even if it took twenty years to fully sink in.

I'm not going anywhere to find God. He is right where I am!

Such Blinding Tact

The small house in Alexandria, west of Glasgow, was the scene for an informal midweek evening house meeting. I was flustered when an exceedingly pretty raven-haired young lady consistently refused to take a chorus sheet from me, in spite of several attempts.

All she would say so sweetly was, 'No thank you . . . No thank you.' She did not open her eyes, but was evidently in that state of smiling ecstasy so well known to swaying charismatics.

I am nothing if not persistent.

As the visiting speaker complete with my customary travelling singer-guitarist, I wanted her to have our own superb *Hallelujah* song sheet. So I kept on insisting. A deadly hush had descended by the time the local leader finally whispered to me, 'She is blind, Maurice . . .'

Oh my goodness, I did feel bad!

But the dark beauty, still smiling, whispered comfortingly, 'It's all right, Maurice, it's all right' and then started to giggle.

I turned to Dave for help. 'Play something quickly!' I pleaded.

My persistency is only matched at times by Dave's guileless artistry. He proved it all too well on this occasion by innocently starting to sing a song which we had recently learned together in a house meeting (in Paris of all places, if that is of any interest. We are nothing if not cosmopolitan!) :

'Open our eyes Lord, we want to see Jesus!'

Feeling bad turned to feeling awful.

But one look at the angelic face of the young blind girl swept all embarrassment away. She was now laughing uncontrollably.

A Colourful Wretch

In spite of being popular in front of an audience I have always suffered from horrendous nervous problems. Many is the time I have rushed out to a basin, retching violently before a performance. As yet I have not vomited on stage, but I have come close, much too close. Of course, it is not a big deal. We can always clear it up! Or so I jest if under extreme pressure and feel the need to confess to my listeners.

In spite of my attempts to pass the malady off with humour, it is nevertheless a painful business and has caused endless distress over many years. Never more so than one day a long time ago when I was invited to the small town of Cobham in Surrey for a week-long series of meetings.

'A Colourful Speaker from Kent' announced the confident poster outside the hall.

By the time I was on my feet I was a bag of nerves and endeavouring to comfort myself with the familiar words of St Paul the Apostle : 'I was not among you with excellency of speech, but in fear and trembling . . .' However it did not work. I felt utterly wretched. I was definitely going to be sick this time. The room was beginning to swim round and round, whilst I struggled to concentrate my mind and remain coherent. I was a long way short of colourful and felt as pale as death.

'Perhaps someone could bring me a chair?' I quipped. 'I will be all right. I can carry on. I am just feeling a little unwell, that's all.' Things had never reached these proportions before, but I kept talking.

It was then I seemed to hear a quiet parallel voice

inside my head and this intruder was quoting poetry. 'I must be going off my rocker!' I thought, now adding a third voice to the duet.

Still! continuing my platform dissertation concerning the 'on-high calling of God' I could clearly discern a couple of lines repeating themselves over and over inside my head. I vaguely guessed they harped back to schooldays and were possibly from 'The Boy Stood on the Burning Deck', but I have never bothered to check it out.

> 'And when his legs were smitten off
> He fought upon his stumps . . .'

The truth dawned. 'That's what I am doing. I am fighting on my stumps!' With the realisation of defeat I glanced imploringly at Ted, my fellow traveller and he knew it was time to take over and clambered to my side. I had finished my superconcentrated drivel.

It was a far cry from the Apostle's glorious ending to his quotation about weakness: '. . . and in evidence of the Spirit's power!' Maybe my time would come later? Meanwhile I would just retch along as best I could.

Book Review: 1

If you suffer from nervous anticipation, it can be a tense time waiting to begin a public oration. Not so bad of course if every one is singing along happily so one can wait and then stand up when feeling full of divine unction. However not all chairmen are free enough to allow such a compassionate approach. In fact many seem obsessed with drawing out the agony until the very last moment, when they express great pleasure in calling upon the nervous wreck beside them.

Of major assistance in this prolongation is the time-honoured tradition of reviewing the books on the bookstall. Some are so verbose and adept at this in-depth procedure as to render any subsequent purchase quite superfluous. The first meeting of a weekend addressing one hundred students from the London University Christian Union will serve to illustrate more than adequately.

My colleague and fellow speaker on this occasion was renowned for rescuing dire situations. Once I heard him utter a closing prayer when a meeting had only been in progress for a few minutes; he decided it was too awful to be allowed to continue. His skill was never more tested than on this occasion.

As the academic young chairman droned on, holding up book after book for nigh on half an hour, the heads of the audience sank lower and lower. When everyone was at their very lowest ebb he shamelessly called upon us to address the drooping undergraduates. I looked desperately across at my friend and indicated I could not possibly follow this introduction. He accepted the awesome challenge with a wry smile and walked solemnly towards the lectern.

Upon arriving he paused and stared for what seemed an interminable age. The absolute silence seemed to have the effect of building a platform of anticipation from which he could speak. When the construction was ready he turned slowly to the chairman and said with great deliberation:

'Well . . . Thank you, brother!'

The whole place shook with laughter and we were back on course for a good meeting. Maybe it wasn't particularly kind, but it was effective.

Come to think of it, we all addressed each other as 'brother' in those days, rather similar to a Communist rally or a Trade Union meeting, I suppose; but we thought nothing of it. In fact the mode of address became so commonplace that for a period we even reduced it to 'bro'!

It all seems like a bad dream now and I am relieved to have friends with forenames again. It is so easy to pick up these funny habits.

Book Review: 2

An extremely kind older friend, who for many years ran a guesthouse in a picturesque port in the West Country, was the undisputed Grandmaster of Book Reviewers. Some time back it was common practice for many evangelical Christians to take a holiday there and get a meeting every evening thrown in, plus two on Sunday for good measure. The stories of our host's reviews became quite legendary, until by repute there was no time for the meeting at all.

The compassionate, but over-devil-conscious, guesthouse owner was also at his most devastating when adding a monotone warning not to visit the evil Witches' House in a nearby resort. His description was so lurid that the assembled company was divided equally between those who were so frightened that it tended to spoil their holiday, and those who were so intrigued they could not wait to get there.

Many a speaker has died a death trying to follow the grandmaster.

After his departure in retirement to the United States, legend further has it that (in true London Bridge style) an American has bought the Witches' House and is transporting it stone by stone across the pond.

I have not been able to substantiate this rumour to date, but it would be delightfully wicked to think that the unabridged monotone warnings could now be inflicted upon another nation. Perhaps with the odd book review?

Since commencing these stories I have learned that our genial host has gone to his eternal resting place, and I am sure he is big enough and has time enough to smile down on our ruminations—unless of course they have books up there!

To the Death

'**H**ave you seen the advert for Arthur's book in *Ripened Grain* this month?" someone asked me.

'No,' I replied.

'It's worth a look!' the farmer's wife smiled at me as she dashed off for a copy.

There it was:

'GOD'S CHOSEN FAST—A MUST FOR THE HUNGRY CHRISTIAN.'

How do we do it?

Easily I suppose.

I would love to add that the book review was by Pastor Way, but that would be too loosely based on truth. However I did *know* of a Pastor Way—and a Canon Ball crossed my path at the cathedral!

Stop me before I continue about the church elder Mr Onions, who always insisted he was Mr. OH-NIGH-ONS. And of course the Rev B'stard whose name was spelled differently, and . . . well you know your own I am sure.

I feel sure I would have rushed for a deed poll.

Kerry *Who?*

Not all planning meetings are an unmitigated disaster, but the possibility is always there. Let me go back a good many years and introduce the preparation for the proposed Roman Catholic and House Churches Combined Worship Meeting, to be staged at grandiose Westminster Central Hall in the centre of London. As an acknowledged expert in the field of free charismatic worship, Yours Truly was approached to lead the great occasion and teach the uninitiated Catholics how to 'Flow in the Spirit'.

'Right up my street' I muttered to myself confidently.

I agreed to attend a seemingly unnecessary planning meeting held just down the road at that huge red brick edifice, the Westminster Cathedral. What did we need to plan? Surely I would just play it by ear as usual, with no written or unwritten liturgy to guide me. If I raised my arms then the capacity crowd would assuredly rise as one man. Whatever I sang out, then our own accomplished musicians would pick up instantly and even alter the key if necessary. Of course, if I pitched in D then I had an endless repertoire at my disposal and could flow from one song to another with consummate ease. Where was the problem?

The chief liaison officer was a Protestant Colonel who introduced me to an august array of about a dozen clergy seated around an impressive oak table. Planning was obviously a serious business. He announced that I would need to have a free hand if the meeting was to be as spontaneous as everyone seemed to want it to be. He then handed everyone a list of the contributors and startled me completely with a loud official clearing of the throat, continuing somewhat in the following vein:

'So if you come on at seven o'clock, Maurice, and lead the worship until the Bishop is introduced at 7.03 . . .'

'Three minutes?' I gasped, totally gob-smacked.

'There will be a green light just ahead of you. When that turns to red you have one minute to round off . . .'

'But . . . we might carry on for half an hour before . . .'

'I will be behind you on the platform with a control button . . .'

'But Colonel . . .'

'The Bishop will finish at 19.07 and you can lead more worship until 19.10, when Father Murphy will introduce the Birmingham Orchestra.'

'But couldn't we just continue in worship until someone feels the moment is right . . . ?'

'Oh dear no! Our Catholic friends are not used to that . . .'

'But you said . . .'

'After the orchestra has finished at 19.17 then Father Callaghan will introduce *Kyrie Eleison*.'

By this time my blood heat had risen considerably. I felt trapped and conned. Any moment he could be telling me be sure to stand to attention at the microphone and to synchronise watches at regular intervals!

Perhaps I just didn't listen properly, for by this time I was thoroughly sick of the heavy organisation, and particularly with everyone being formally introduced instead of wandering on in our usual spontaneous manner. Anyway I had stomached enough and decided to challenge the meeting eyeball to eyeball.

'Why does *Kyrie Eleison* have to be introduced?' I

demanded. 'Can't she just walk straight on and sing when she is ready?'

The overloaded silence shouted aloud my ignorance. The heavy cloistered surroundings seemed to close in even more as the terrifying stillness declared I had said something awfully wrong. My blood ran cold and I sat at the head of the table feeling absolutely dreadful. What innocent blunder could cause such an atmosphere? Maybe this Kyrie was not the same Antipodean lady that so masterfully sang the *Chants d'Auverne*?

'Well . . . ?' I enquired in a weak voice.

Give him his due, the Colonel shouldered the weight of responsibility. 'Hmm! . . .' He cleared his throat again and spoke very slowly.

'*Kyrie Eleison* is Greek for "Lord Have Mercy", Maurice.'

'Oh!'

I thrashed around in my mind trying to find some face-saving way out. Glancing at the typewritten programme my eye caught sight of the words '*Agnus Dei*'. By some stroke of providence I knew this was one more of those darned Greek quotations and not another woman called Agnes! (I have checked up since for safety's sake and found that it actually means 'Lamb of God'; but I am sure you know that.)

I decided to try it on.

'I saw *Agnus Dei* was singing later,' I quipped, stressing the Agnes and laughing falsely, endeavouring to draw them all in.

Like the greatly renowned Sovereign before them, they were not amused. At this point I realised with horror that they had completely missed the joke and thought I was being serious about Agnes. This House

Church heathen obviously did not even know the rudiments of religion.

How we scraped through the rest of the evening I do not remember. It was all a kind of yellow mist from then on. But what I do know is that as I stood before the masses on the night, gazing up at the painted dome in the great hall, I sensed my public days were numbered and a 'still small voice' was gently persisting:

'Leave it out, Maurice! Your days on the big stage are finished.'

I obeyed, and have not stepped out of the wings for the past ten years or so; but no doubt the charismatic bandwaggon is rolling along very nicely without their spontaneous worship leader. It always takes me a long time to realise that Big God can really manage these jobs without the help of Little Me.

Prayer Boon in Westminster

The musical *Come Together* was being held at the Westminster Central Hall narrated by the world-famous Pat Boone. He did a great job till it came to the spontaneous bit where the leader can act as he feels led.

'If two of you shall agree as touching anything . . .' he exhorted as I listened to this doubtful exegesis. He got carried away even further stating that as there were two thousand of us present, 'how much more' would God answer?

I sighed and looked across at my friend John beside me. We had often stood side by side on the same platfrom leading charismatic meetings of the same ilk.

'But we must be agreed, nothing between us' flowed out from the microphone; 'If you have anything against anyone in this hall then get up from your seat and go to them now and put it right!'

There was movement everywhere as John and I sat rooted to our seats. We were obviously likely to hold up this mighty move of God.

Suddenly I was aware that there were about ten people forming a queue in front of me.

'I have never liked you, Maurice,' said the first. 'I just wanted to confess that to you.'

Well thanks.

'I have always hated you, Maurice!' said the next without any evident sign of sorrow over the fact.

Much appreciated.

'I can't stand the way you lead the worship,' said another.

Thanks again. This is doing me the power of good.

A glance at John showed his face wreathed in smiles. No one had come to him. Perhaps they felt he would give them an earful in return—he was always more forthright than me.

Eventually my dissenters ran out and I noticed everyone else was returning to their seats too.

Thank goodness that is over.

As the hubbub subsided Pat began to pray for specific requests now that we were all in 'one accord'. Well I wasn't, I can assure you; I was feeling wounded and resentful.

Then he had a moment of inspiration. He would open the microphone up to anyone from the audience who had a prayer that we could all agree about.

That was the signal for every aspiring platform-lover to rush forward.

I am sad to say that we had all sorts of people 'saved' that night, and I jest not when I tell you that the most significant was Mao Tse Tung himself. But I don't think he knew anything about it.

We may possibly have been as innocent as doves, but were certainly not as wise as serpents on this occasion.

Come to think of it, after all those piercing remarks that came my way I am not so sure about the innocent either!

The Gate of Heaven

Picture the elders closeted on another occasion, this time at the seaside town of Deal and awaiting the arrival of the Big White Chief from the London centre.

The place we sat in was about ten feet long and three feet wide at most. We sat huddled in a row with our faces close to the opposite wall, where our noses made frequent contact with brooms and mops that were suspended from hooks.

It was in fact the broom cupboard. The corrugated iron meeting house, although ornately furnished with cinema seats and a long red carpet runner, was very small. This cupboard was the best place we could manage for the leaders to meet apart from the plebeians.

We were trying to appear dignified awaiting our visitor from his splendid premises in South London.

Eventually came a hesitant knock and then the door was opened wide.

There he stood appraising us before he spoke.

'I know what Jacob meant now, when he said of Bethel: "This is the gate of heaven and a dreadful place!" '

Well I was not sure about the former, but the latter was certainly true.

The Word of Ministry

The local conference gave an opportunity for those of lesser calibre to mix with the top brass from The Centre in London. Sometimes we might even be permitted to give the ministry at one session if everyone was convinced of our divine unction on the day.

The elders were closeted and seeking guidance concerning who would speak, which was tricky because we all knew everyone wanted to hear the big man himself. It seemed to me he also thought he was the best equipped.

I had a sense of something important burning in me and felt this was my chance to grab the limelight. Of course I would never have admitted it then, maybe did not even recognise the fact.

'Who has the word of the Lord then?' the important man enquired.

'I have a word,' I said gravely, hoping to impress.

He inclined his head slowly in my direction and spoke with deliberation:

'A word. It is not *a* word we want, brother. It is *The Word*!'

Well, that was me finished.

Anyone who spoke in public after that had better come up with the goods.

I am certain that admonition, and the years spent in such an atmosphere, contributed to the great lack of confidence which followed me whenever I went to address any group of people. Still does to this day.

After all, would it be good enough? Would it be *The Word*?

A Ripe Story

Recently visiting the USA I encountered a man who showed impatience with the Christian scene as I chatted with him.

'I'm up to here with 'em!' he explained, holding his hand alongside the top of his head.

Of course I gently enquired the cause of his concern.

'So damned insensitive,' he stated willingly. 'Do you know I took the Chief Executive of our company to a Christian Businessmen's luncheon and was made to look a proper fool?'

The story took no dragging from him. His CE was a quiet retiring man and had steadfastly refused invitations to these gregarious occasions. However, having been assured that this particular meeting was to be an undemonstrative occasion, he had apprehensively agreed to come along. As long as my friend could assure him he would not be 'got at'.

Having primed all the eager beavers that his boss did not want converting and should be left to come along at his own pace, the employee turned up at the hotel and ushered the company leader inside.

On opening the restaurant doors he saw to his astonishment that everyone was wearing a huge cardboard banana. Before he could turn and protect his boss, someone had rushed up and thrown his arms round the man, grappling him in a kind of charismatic bearhug and then slapped a self-adhesive banana sticker on his lapel.

'Come on in and join the bunch!' everyone chorused.

That was it. They lost two bananas that day!

Well, we import most things from over that side of the pond and I wonder how long it will be before the fruit arrives.

'Never!' you say?

Don't you bet on it!

In the Post Office?

My other infamous friend who rescued me from the lair of those boring book reviews reported upon elsewhere used to put the matter so succinctly when he was asked that dreadful perennial question, 'Where do you worship?'

'Well . . .' he would reply, so light-of-heart, 'In the Post Office, the supermarket . . . and Woolworths!'

Such internal freedom did not prevent him from worshipping with other people if he wanted to, but it was no longer mandatory. He did not fear a black mark for non-attendance. God was where he was.

(I just seem to recall a certain woman who had had many husbands and was presently living with someone who was not on this list, desperately trying to evade the issue that Jesus was confronting her with. She endeavoured to sidetrack Him with 'Our fathers worshipped in this mountain.' Talking about *where* can often save us from talking about *who*. The Master of course had none of it and told her gently but firmly, that 'in spirit and truth' was where the worship business was at.)

Of course, I am sure that God can be found in cathedral, chapel or garret meeting—in fact anywhere; but surely nowhere unless first of all within the human heart?

Immanuel, God with us.

A Fly in the Ointment

So this was France then. Or 'bloody abroad' as my father would have it. Perhaps I'll encounter more reality beyond Calais?

We were a small team from the local church who had bravely crossed the Channel and were now engaged in a mission to a tiny village in the northern part of Brittany. The inhabitants no doubt had a small team engaged in a similar mission somewhere in Britain, but then exchange is no robbery. We had enjoyed some good times with the natives, and in spite of my lack of French ('Don't speak a word of the language, old boy!'), we'd had what we felt were profound exchanges.

Our hosts responded by inviting us to join with them in a service of communion. The church's whitewashed walls were rather bleak, and the stark furniture consisted of a single circle of wooden-backed chairs with raffia seats. In the centre of these stood a plain table, clothed very decently in a white damask tablecloth. A shallow basket contained half a metre of French bread (naturally!) and a simple, but nonetheless silver cup held a rich-looking red *Chateau Special*.

We took our places and as the service progressed in French, I suppressed a naughty subconscious suspicion that God was probably English. Some things are pretty universal though, I mused, as a large fly buzzed uninvited through the open window and landed deliberately on the clean white tablecloth. I wondered what the

French would call it. '*Bouteille bleu*' perhaps?

As we watched, transfixed by such a small matter, the fly crawled the whole length of the bread, only stopping occasionally, seemingly to rub its legs together. I was glad the bread had been round already.

The unholy intruder moved to the chalice and paused on the lip. Though intermittently closing their eyes to murmur their worship, most of the assembled company were also warily watching the fly to make sure it didn't fall in. The insect then leant over into the cup and began a perilous vertical descent towards the wine. The eyes of everyone present grew rounder. Next we heard a soft, wet buzz, more of a fizz really, as when a candle is extinguished between a wet finger and thumb. The inevitable had happened.

No one moved. No one spoke. Certainly no one got up and fished the thing out. I couldn't believe what was happening, for each single person was seemingly caught up in a common tacit understanding so often observed during accidents at times of extreme seriousness: we will all pretend it hasn't happened!

The leader stood and picked up the chalice. 'Oh good,' I thought. 'Now's his chance.' But no! After yet one more prayer, he presented the container to one of the communicants on the far side of the circle.

Once again the eyes grew even rounder, as each participant drank (but very, very carefully) and passed the cup on.

'Why are they all pretending?' I thought, determined that when the wine reached me, I would discreetly but deftly deal with the problem. I need not have bothered to come to such a momentous decision, for when the cup did finally reach me, the fly had gone.

Had I but dared and had we been in England I would have chosen the next hymn: 'There was an old lady who swallowed a fly . . .' Ten to one God would have joined in?

Too Soon We Rise

Picture if you can a Sunday Brethren Assembly. Two solemn elders in dark attire, seated one each end of a bench in a sparse cold meeting room on a wintry sabbath morning, face an equally sober square of worshippers. On the bench, beside the older of the two rests the bread and the wine—the symbols—that will soon be passed reverently from hand to hand, once the lengthy prayers are finished.

At long last the divine communing is over and all is absolutely silent. We await the inevitable slow deliberate and reverential rising of Elder Number One.

Unfortunately he is so absorbed with due solemnity that he forgets to take hold of the symbols. Or perhaps he was intending to turn and bend for them? Or maybe both men were intending to rise at the same time, and one moved too soon? Perhaps the bench was usually filled with elders? We don't know.

What is sure and even more unfortunate is that his Number Two was perched at the very far end of the bench, which meant that immediately the old man rose all the weight was concentrated at this extremity.

You have guessed right. It could not have been rehearsed more perfectly for a slapstick comedy.

Number Two sank completely to the floor as the bench tipped forty-five degrees and the bread and wine slid the full length and ended up covering the second-in-command and finally clattering to the floor in total disarray.

Oh dear, whatever happened to the holy atmosphere? But what a dire temptation to follow with the familiar eucharistic closing hymn:
'Too soon we rise; the symbols disappear;
The feast, though not the love, is past and gone;'
Too soon indeed!

Nip and Sip

Our 'Honor Oak*-style' Breaking of Bread service had all the appearance of a competition to see who could break off the smallest morsel of bread. This was immediately followed by the regular drinking-the-teeniest-drop-of-nonalcoholic-wine competition, effected miraculously from thimble-sized glasses.

A very far cry from the 'Last Supper' from which our feast was supposed to draw its inspiration. Also in such contrast to the wedding scene where our extravagant Lord saved the situation by turning a vast gallonage of water into fermented wine. No spoilsport He!

'The nip and the sip' was accompanied by a rather strange period of time marked out by the continual sound of ecstatic murmuring :

'Amen' . . . 'Praise the Lord' . . . 'Mmm' . . . 'Yes' . . . 'Glory to God' . . .

All this with both eyes firmly closed, as we were supposed to be 'Remembering the Lord', to use the in club jargon.

Week after week this proved too much of a trial and my mind would start to wander, particularly if Arsenal had lost the day before, which was much more of a tragedy than a spiritual elder like me would care to admit. One sure way to get yourself into a heap of condemnation is to think about your favourite football team when your thoughts should be resolutely fixed on the ultimate sacrifice .

Personally, I am deeply grateful for that 'Hill Far

---

* Honor Oak was the title attributed to our church grouping, derived from the name of the suburb of London in which the first meeting was staged.

Away', but I've learned through the years that the Almighty is not the hard taskmaster we made Him out to be. I cannot prove that He really supports those magnificent 'Gunners' who inspire the faithful on the Highbury Stadium terraces, but I am quite certain He does not disapprove of my enthusiasm which sometimes invades my sacred moments.

After all, my quiet enthusiasm for Him is with me all day, every day; and sometimes trying to focus that to order, and sense His divine presence, can result in quite the opposite effect. So I have found.

Of course, at other times my enthusiasm for Him boils over and I am blessed out of my red and white socks!

When 'El Vino' Won at Derby

Perhaps the time when I was most deeply touched by the mysterious administration of the consecrated elements was at an Anglican eucharist in Derby. Here I found reality in the raw.

I had been asked to give a twenty-minute sermon, whereas in the circles in which I moved one rarely spoke for less that one hour. (Was it John Wesley who said that if a man can say what he has to say in twenty minutes, he shouldn't say it at all?)

As I entered the building I noticed that the whole rear portion of the church had been boarded off to give a place of shelter to down-and-outs, alcoholics and others with unfortunate circumstances. The large, clearly ebullient vicar greeted me effusively and said with a wide smile, 'Come in here, Maurice, while I put my frock on!'

As we emerged still chatting and laughing from the vestry, I noticed a huge garishly blue plastic baptistery had been erected in the side aisle, while a scruffy black and white dog slept contentedly beneath the table from which I was to speak.

After the solemn preliminaries I approached the makeshift pulpit in time to hear an old lady mutter to her companion, 'Last time I'm coming, my dear. They've even got dogs in 'ere now!'

The vicar expressed his delight with my decently short homily and spontaneously invited me to join him in administering the sacrament. I was extremely surprised as I supposed I was not a *bona fide* cleric, and then quite overcome as I viewed the long snake of a line which extended down the chancel steps, the whole length of the nave and continued out of sight along the back of the church. There was no attempt to usher the congregation forward by rows, and in the resulting usual dribs and drabs; everyone was left to their own devices. The whole church was on the move, there was life in the place. I noticed with approval the evident mixture of social classes and became even more 'strangely moved' (as a good Wesleyan would say).

I was at a loss for words and that is something unusual. 'What shall I say?' I asked the vicar tentatively.

'You take the cup, give it to everyone and say whatever you like,' he replied, with his usual wide grin illuminating the area behind the altar rail.

The sight of this great mixed bag of both fortunate and unfortunate humanity, all waiting to be served, contrived to affect my emotions. Tears were already misting my eyes as I addressed the first communicant.

Thinking of Christ's unstinting sacrifice, and that He would have come to give His life had there only been just one to save, I looked compassionately at the first participant, an elderly man who shuffled forward with outstretched arms and upturned hands. Looking him straight in the eyes I whispered emotionally, 'All for you!'

Upon these words he sipped gratefully from the great silver chalice as huge tears began to roll down his weatherbeaten face. I gulped involuntarily and moved on saying gently to the next in line, 'All for you!'

The evidently well-to-do lady sipped in genteel fashion and then visibly broke down.

'There's going to be a Revival!' I thought.

A few more folks, young and old alike, came forward

and felt the impact of the power from on high, by which
time I was beginning to enjoy the evident unction and
almost cockily approached a young woman who looked
sadly down-at-heel.

'All . . . for . . . you, my love,' I said with calculated
benevolence, and waited for the inevitable response.

She eyed the brimming chalice with alarm for several seconds and then blurted out with a voice that all
around could hear, 'Wot! all of it?'

The atmosphere was instantly dispersed. Everything
was spoiled. There were no more tears. Hundreds of
earnest souls came and went as I stood dazed behind the
rail tragically endeavouring to speak a few meaningful
words.

I took my leave of the radical Derby Anglicans pondering upon the mysteries of divine unction, feeling I
had a long way to go before I ministered with the
Master's purity of heart.

Perhaps one day, a few more miles along the painful
road of experience, I'll get there.

Total Immersion

As I look back to the many baptisms I have witnessed or participated in, I am always painfully reminded of the inevitable vulnerability of total immersion.

My first-ever experience was to mark out the pattern; what biblical scholars might call, 'The law of first occurrences'! The actual dunking was preceded by my overlong and intensely serious exposition on the symbolic nature of the ceremony.

'This is a *burial*,' I stated to the motley assembly of believers of all ages, gathered solemnly around a child's frail swimming pool in a friend's back garden on a midsummer's day. 'It is off with the old, and on with the new! We are dead to the old way of living!'

I continued to enthuse, 'You will not live your own life any more after this! This is your burial!'

A strapping longhaired Flower Power hippie-type young man who possessed a heart of gold but was not exactly a contestant for *Brain of Britain* obviously failed to fully comprehend my religious drift.

I heard him turn to my son and whisper with the utmost concern, ' 'Ere, Dave, 'ow long does 'e 'old us under?'

I could justly be charged with many offences against humanity during ultrareligious years, but thankfully murder is not one of them.

Accidental death? Well nearly I am afraid, as we have sometimes struggled to recover overweight candidates in too many clothes from too high seas. I remember it was guaranteed to raise the enjoyment level of local holidaymakers, themselves usually struggling with the wet English summer climate. We were probably better than Punch and Judy!

Penguin on Parade

Not all sacraments are informal of course.

Once, whilst visiting Farnborough in Hampshire, as I stood waiting to give the final message of the day, I saw my friend the Baptist minister slip quietly out to change, ready to baptise a new member.

He emerged in long black rubber waders which encased him completely to the waist, making it almost impossible for him to walk.

As he waddled like a penguin towards the sunken tank I struggled ineffectively to keep a straight face. It is the only time I have laughed all through the sacrament.

He later told me, that having caught sight of my initial look of horror as he shuffled from the vestry, he purposed he would never wear the outfit again.

So I venture to say that we accomplished some good that evening.

On the Catwalk

Of course with so much water around one should never neglect the safety factor. Thus I was exhorted before visiting an East Kent branch of the Fellowship of Independent Evangelical Churches.

They had invested in a splendid new sunken baptistery which had a catwalk leading to the centre of the pool, from which one could dramatically address the congregation and those waiting to be immersed. On this occasion I was chosen to preach and my two fellow-elders were to lower the candidates into the tank.

Straightening my best Sunday suit I made a stately promenade to the centre island and launched into my usual fervent discourse on the symbolic sacrament of our death and resurrection. I concluded with a final flourish of rhetoric and outstretched arms.

Completely carried away and forgetting that I was surrounded by water, the inevitable happened. I closed my Bible dramatically, turned sharply to the right and walked off . . . but literally.

The next second I was well over my waist in water and the seriousness of the moment was entirely lost as a stupefied gasp ran throughout the whole church.

Nobody dared to laugh openly, but the sniggering eventually surfaced, along with the overeager orator, and continued for most of the service. Once out of the holy environs the would-be worshippers were not so restrained.

Maybe with a lot less pomp and circumstance and a touch more simplicity we should have less of these misadventures. And, if we did nevertheless encounter them, perhaps also a touch more honesty would at least ensure a good healthy bout of laughter. An Old Testament text even states it is good for your navel!

If we could have gone that far and lost our fear of dispelling the presence of God with a belly laugh, maybe we should even have encountered Him within the framework of the gift of humour.

But of course, the New Testament never recorded that Jesus actually laughed! Also one of His Apostles is represented as having issued a direct warning against any form of undue levity.

So we did our best not to enjoy ourselves too much, and most especially at meeting times.

A Slip of the Tongue

In every sphere there is always one story that takes the biscuit.

For me, in the matter of dreams and visions, it will always be the relaying to a mixed public audience, in the respectable stockbroker belt of mid-Surrey, of our most important vision.

An identical picture had been received by two people quite unknown to each other. However, they were both known to a common third party.

This 'out of the mouth of two witnesses' vision held great sway among us and encouraged us to hire large venues in the heart of London to hold meetings of jubilant praise. These culminated in a magnificent inspired evening at the Royal Albert Hall, which was filled to its capacity of well over six thousand people, with many turned away.

The vision, believe it or not, was of an octopus spread all over the city, with its tentacles squeezing the life out of the people of God.

Don't ask me how we knew what it meant because I cannot tell you, but each of us was unmistakably convinced that we should gather folks in the nation's capital to offer evenings of praise (never mind a message!) and that many would be released from religiosity into a more free realm of living, as indeed they very soon were.

Some years afterwards, a most enthusiastic orator among us was relating this story to the aforementioned gathering of about five hundred people in Surrey. As he held forth at his usual breakneck speed, an incredible gasp from the audience was followed by a deep embarrassed hush.

Aware that something was gravely amiss he paused in full flow, shielded the microphone from his mouth and spoke sideways to a colleague standing beside him on the platform.

'What has happened?' he whispered in desperation. 'What have I said?'

'You said *testicles*!' his friend replied, struggling to contain his laughter.

No comment.

All Good Gifts

'For to one is given the word of wisdom . . . another the word of knowledge . . . another faith . . . another gifts of healing . . . another the effecting of miracles . . . another prophecy . . . another the distinguishing of spirits . . . another various kinds of tougues . . . another the interpretation of tongues.'

The Apostle Paul

'Oft times the Devil feigneth quaint sounds in their ears, quaint lights and shining in their eyes, and wonderful smells in their noses; and all is but falsehood.'

'The Cloud of Unknowing'
Author unknown

Three Divine Errors

The Charismatic Renewal which invaded the Western world during the sixties brought with it a great deal of excitement and liberation about which volumes have been written.

I (of course!) remember too the excesses, particularly in the realm of the gift of prophecy. Individuals who felt directly inspired by God made utterances in His name, often prefaced by the formal biblical introduction: '*Thus saith the Lord!*'

This made the statement very difficult to argue with, in spite of the Apostle Paul's scriptural injunction to the early church to test such utterances.

Why the King James language was so regularly invoked I have no idea, unless it was thought to add even more authenticity. After all, it is a well-known fact that many earnest Christians believe the Authorised Version to be the one used by St Paul himself!

Some of the more outrageous utterances bear repetition, commencing with the infamous opening statement from the Divine Memory:

'Thus saith the Lord, I have forgotten thy name my son . . .'

Or, when wanting to show God's disapproval and abstinence from the current proceedings:

'I am not here! saith the Lord.'

The use of impressive Old Testament names became quite commonplace too. One such name was *Ichabod* (which being interpreted means 'The glory has departed'). It was used frequently to show (yet again!) almighty and miserable disapproval with the proceedings.

Recently whilst in Florida, I was informed that a slip of the tongue had caused the following utterance to astound the morning devotees:

'Thus saith the Lord, I have written *Michelob* over this place'.

(For the sake of the uninitiated may I labour the humour by telling you that 'Michelob' is the name of a well-known brand of American beer.)

One cannot help but wonder if it was not perhaps a Freudian slip they had all witnessed!

Three Dumb Sheep

Humorous, but most serious, error is exposed when we consider three friends of mine entering a loud praise meeting in a West Country village, where unfortunately the only seats available were right at the front of a packed hall.

Having never seen such extrovert worship before, they sat quietly taking in the proceedings as the instruments blasted *allegro* and one large and very happy lady banged her fists enthusiastically on the door behind her in time with the beat, while just about everyone else danced up and down on the spot (in what later became known as the Charismatic Hop). Everyone sang one short chorus over and over (and over) again.

When eventually the music wound down, the congregation remained on their feet in an expectant silence. In due course the voice of the would-be prophet boomed out:

'Thus saith the Lord, there are three dumb sheep in the midst!'

Thankfully the visitors were secure enough to respond in unison, 'Baa, Baa, Baa!'

But it could have been extremely damaging to the confidence of someone less sure of their acceptance by God Himself.

As in so many of these bizarre instances one is left with the joint desire to both laugh and cry.

Three Things to Say

I well remember that a close friend of mine was responsible for causing one of the loudest groans on record in response to his prophecy.

We were nearing the end of a large public meeting in the heart of London's East End. The atmosphere was electric and no one wanted to waste a second. The prominent wallclock declared we had just twenty minutes left, and the ill-tempered caretaker was hovering ominously near the door with his keys already to hand.

The overall leadership of the meeting was in my hands and I wanted to capitalise on the sense of presence we were experiencing.

'Let us be still before we leave,' I said. 'Maybe there is something else for us to hear tonight. If not, then let us soak up this quietness which is no doubt doing good to our souls.' That, or something similar, caused a further deepening of the stillness.

At this point my friend, well-known for his slow, deliberate and at times lengthy messages rose purposefully to his feet to pronounce:

'Thus saith the Lord, I have three things to say to you, my people.'

He elaborated in archaic Old Testament language and detail for possibly fifteen long minutes, with no sign of concluding. During a brief pause one could hear frustrated but suppressed heavy breathing coming from just about every member of the congregation.

Then he finally blew us all away by looking solemnly around the assembled company and stating confidently:

'Secondly, my people . . .'

Secondly! That was it. The heads went right down. The night was over.

All that detail was almost certainly in great contrast to the biblical messenger Haggai, who stated so simply, 'I am with you, saith the Lord' (Haggai 2:13) . . . and caused a whole nation to rise up and rebuild the Temple of God.

Mind you, in true legalistic form these awesome few words, the total content of the Old Testament prophecy, were taken hold of by many budding aspirants merely to introduce their prophecies. Understandably no one took much notice of those now overused and powerful words,

'I am with you . . .'

But what a great thing, if He really is with us!

Words of Wisdom and Knowledge

It was sheer amazement that greeted the operation of this supernatural 'word of knowledge', presented to a packed auditorium from a London stage:

'There is a man here tonight who came on . . . a number 10 bus from North London! God wants to heal him tonight.'

No response.

'He is sitting on the left-hand side of the auditorium. If he will stand then I will minister to him.'

Still no response. But a very long pause.

'Maybe I am not quite accurate. Is there a lady perhaps . . . ?'

'What about the other side of the hall?'

'Strange! I was sure . . . perhaps I was mistaken . . . Ah yes! A train, that's it . . .'

Yet still no response; except a titter in my row.

We only had South London left, but thankfully our budding miracle worker gave up and decided to try another candidate before crossing the Thames.

I am not doubting the sincerity and am prepared to acknowledge that initially some gifted folk do hear something from that inner voice at times. However, once one has become a semiprofessional and expected to perform to order in public and on stage, there is great pressure to come up with the goods, and great scope for the imagination.

Now and again one may strike lucky. Similarly, if I go out into Trafalgar Square with a machine gun I am quite likely to hit someone, but that does not make me a marksman!

The gifts, 'word of knowledge' and 'word of wisdom', along with others including one labelled 'discerning of spirits', were clearly listed in Paul's letter to his wayward Corinthians. These were willingly embraced by charismatics two millennia later in an endeavour to solve some of the problems and heartaches of living in the final quarter of this cruel twentieth century. A 'word of knowledge' or information obtained from a supernatural source can greatly raise the faith of a timid soul seeking to reach out and obtain a blessing from the Originator of all blessings. No question about it, some have been greatly helped; but as usual the misuse of these gifts has caused many a wry smile, along with many additional heartaches as false hopes were raised and dashed. Perhaps it is better not to try and help the Holy Spirit after all?

Thankfully I cannot recall too many of these absurdities, but I do well remember that 'gifts of discernment', often supposedly revealing the darker side of some poor believer's life, became secretly known among us as 'gifts of suspicion'.

It was amazing what some leaders got away with because they spoke with an authoritarian voice. It is recorded that Jesus spoke with authority, but I think that just means He knew what He was talking about, don't you?

Rally Round the Flag

If the gift of prophecy left room for fertile imagination, much more so that well-explored charismatic realm of dreams and visions. Doubtless there has been a genuine fulfilment of the well-known New Testament prophecy, 'Your young men shall see visions and your old men shall dream dreams'; but who could have foreseen the inventiveness of those earnest young people, all seeking to have a continuing part in the divine outpouring three-quarters of the way through the twentieth century?

Leaving aside the exotic dreams caused by heavy cheese suppers held up as divine intervention, let us merely touch upon some of the incredulous mind pictures optimistically called visions that were often shared within the intensity of a fervent group, seated with eyes closed and all deeply breathing as if inhaling exotic perfume.

Take for outstanding instance the special meeting just north of London:

'I can see an elephant . . . and it is balancing on a tightrope . . .' announced the swaying young man, his eyelids clamped firmly together and his brow furrowed deeply 'Yes . . . I can see now . . . it is holding a Union Jack in its trunk!'

Oh my goodness! Such an utterance is enough to clean-bowl any chance the meeting ever had.

On this occasion my quickwitted companion once again redeemed the situation with a hearty:

'*Praise God, the circus has come to town!*'

Which interjection reduced the tense assembly to

shrieks of laughter, but I fear did not help the unfortunate seer very much. However, what else could he do?

In fact the Apostle Peter is recorded as having a vision whilst in a trance and they are not too popular in orthodox circles these days! He was on a rooftop and his wide screen revealed a sheet with unclean animals being lowered.

That's a bit way out too I guess; but at least he understood what it meant!

Table d'Hôte

Of course not all picture-revelations were outlandish, but I assure you that a good proportion came into this category. Consider with me now the 'vision' given on an important occasion to the large and highly successful group in Bradford, who were entertaining a prominent speaker from the United States.

The leader told me afterwards how much he had regretted not warning a member of the congregation against having one of his outrageous pictures-in-the-mind.

Sure enough, they had not progressed far into the sanctified hour when the visionary buried his head in his hands and blurted out:

'I can see a place laid for a meal, but instead of a fork I see a spear; instead of a knife I see a hammer. On the plate is a large crab in its shell and also a live eel . . .'

Well, thank you very much! What do we do now? Who on earth is going to interpret that for the edification of the multitude?

After an extremely long and obviously embarrassed silence, the visitor rose slowly and began to interpret. Had they all misjudged their earnest young exponent after all? Did the great man from over the sea possess greater insight into these spiritual matters?

'Three things I say to you,' the American began seriously. 'Take the spear and thrust it through the head of the eel! . . . Take the hammer and crush the crab! . . . And take the young man who gave that vision and forbid him ever to have another like that again!'

Whew! Saved once more.

But something inside me still rebels against having to take such drastic action. There must surely have been a more gentle way to deal with such imaginative and intense participants, however misguided; but unfortunately none of us had mastered the art.

Perhaps it required more compassion than we possessed?

'Transport All Divine'
(courtesy of hymn-writer W. Robinson)

The term 'Transportation in the Spirit' was frequently bandied about among us early charismatics. No doubt this was encouraged by stories we had heard of the famous Bible-smuggler Brother Andrew, who was reported by many to have been 'transported', without the passage of time, from one city behind the Iron Curtain to another. This echoed a similar story attributed to the missionary Gladys Aylward operating in a dangerous situation in China much earlier in this century, and of course there is the famous original counterpart recorded in the Acts of the Apostles.

Now I have no argument with any of this, but become increasingly convinced that such happenings cannot be brought about by human will or desire. But it is tempting to have a go, isn't it? With our snatch-a-text background, a useful example might be, 'Jesus is the same yesterday, today and forever.'

Such an attitude seems to have been prevailing some years back, when after a prayer meeting which had lasted till midnight, a close friend of mine missed the last bus and was stranded in Canterbury. It was eighteen miles from his home by the seaside and he was not a car-owner, yet he resolutely refused a proffered lift.

'You go on home,' he insisted brightly. 'Maybe I shall be lifted up!'

Some days later we enquired how he got on.

'Very well!' he replied; but deeper enquiry revealed that he had walked six miles before a lone motorist stopped and offered him a lift. By this time it was approaching two o'clock.

With a twinkle in his eye he related how the hours had flown past. First of all he had spent the time wondering how best to approach the problem. Should he sit down in the road and await some magic-carpet treatment, or should he just keep walking and see what happened? Thankfully he had decided upon the latter option.

He told us that, astonishingly for such a time of night, the driver of his mercy vehicle was going right to his home town. In fact he was dropped at his own front door, and was sure God had provided for him.

We were not so sure, but nevertheless glad he got a lift home. Surely he would have got the ride if he had just left a poker game?

Well . . . is the Almighty sitting up there somewhere and ordering these divine taxis on an invisible radiophone? To be honest I really don't know; but after all these years I still really do believe some folks have been lifted up and transported. But I have no problem at all if you think I am off my rocker.

However, rest assured, I am not about to sit down in the middle of the road to prove my point.

Gentian Violet

You will have to be patient in order to make the connection between a sick bay in Aldershot barracks and the charismatic persuasion.

I had reported sick to avoid church parade—I had better things to do. However one had to be careful to avoid getting what was known as a 'red ink entry' in your pay book, for this meant the Medical Officer had decided you were malingering. One glance at that and the Platoon Sergeant made sure your life was not worth living.

With the aid of a mysterious earache I had succeeded, but not before being recommended for treatment which apparently entailed funnelling some liquid into my hearing organ.

Whilst I sat awaiting attention by the Lance-Corporal medical orderly, I noticed the preponderance of a violet-coloured liquid. The man next to me had his feet submerged in it, whilst opposite at the sink another soldier was gargling with a similar preparation. Yet another had it painted on to the sores on his arms. True enough, the huge container was to be the obnoxious solution to my problem also!

The junior noncommissioned officer approached with the general-purpose remedy and began syphoning it into my ear.

'Is this all the same stuff?' I queried.

'Oh yes, Gentian Violet!' he replied. 'We use it for most things.'

I was amazed, but mine was not to reason why.

Many, many years later I did begin to reason why

when I noticed many religious folk who had had a particular experience began retailing it as though it was the cure for all the ills of every person they contacted.

It all smacked a little of intolerance, ignorance, and a lack of respect for the unique pathway of another. I noticed that anyone who dared to express that they had any kind of spiritual ailment was almost sure to get the Gentian Violet.

If demons were the current obsession you had them. If being self-centred was dish of the day with the leaders, this was your problem.

And of course, once the amateur psychiatrists got hold of 'in' terms like rejection and inner healing, you were a candidate for months of intense spiritual violet treatment. It saved any diagnosis.

Saddest fact of all perhaps, is that I was for many years almost a major wholesaler for this type of treatment. What I had just experienced you needed.

But no more. I know less and less these days, but as I may have said elsewhere I feel more and more secure in my uncertainty.

*Deaf*initely Healed

Sybil had suffered much in her life, but always retained a sense of humour. One of her many trials was an illness that gave pain in many parts of the body; this added to a deafness which had intensified with the years to the current chronic problem.

One night in a small country town in Hampshire, there was an FGBMFI (Full Gospel Businessmen International) dinner arranged at the local hotel. The visiting speaker was from Eastern Europe and had a reputation for having a healing ministry. Ever hopeful, our friend Sybil went along to listen and participate.

At one point the preacher, who spoke English with a rather pronounced accent, started to give what had become known in the trade as 'words of knowledge'—these being snippets of supernaturally revealed information which often raised hope and faith in the recipients.

'There is a person here, aged about thirty, with a pain across the shoulders,' announced the speaker in his peculiar speaking manner.

After an embarrassing pause, the preacher repeated the invitation. Still nobody moved. Sybil, in order to lip-read more easily, moved forward to another chair. On the third invitation Sybil unravelled the dialect sufficiently to make out the words '. . . in the shoulder', and although in her late fifties, she stepped boldly forward and threaded her way through the tables. An audible gasp went up from the audience.

Once out front the minister could not make her clearly understand what he was saying (a combination of his language impediment and her own lack of hearing). 'I am deaf,' she declared. 'I am deaf!' As the cause of the confusion dawned he indicated he would pray for the ears first, and removed both hearing aids which immediately gave off a high-pitched whistle. Not knowing what to do with the offending objects he passed them to the man leading the meeting. He did not know how to control them either and in an attempt to muffle the whistle clasped them tightly in his hands, which automatically doubled the volume of the high-pitched note. With an expression of abject fear he started to juggle them up and down as though he expected them to explode at any minute. Finally Sybil's husband was able to push his way forward, grab both the hearing aids and defuse them.

The wife of the meeting leader was standing at the side of the meeting. At this point she started to slide slowly down the wall clutching her stomach. Wondering what malady had suddenly struck her, two attendants rushed to her aid and found she was suffering from a fit of suppressed but uncontrollable laughter.

Meanwhile, undaunted by the interruption, our intrepid healer clapped both his hands on Sybil's head and began to pray aloud fervently. He then told Sybil he was going to stand behind her and speak. This was to discover if she could now hear.

The diners' eyes and ears were riveted on the scene. He put his mouth close to her head and everyone leaned forward, expecting a whisper.

'ONE!!' he bellowed at the top of his voice.

Sybil thought she heard something (who wouldn't?) and quietly offered:

'One?'

The healer man was clearly delighted and shouted again:

'TWO!!'

'Two?' she queried again.

'Hallelujah! . . . THREE!!'

'Three!' she said, now bearing a confident smile. And as he stood behind her silently with his hands aloft in triumph, Sybil went right on: 'Four . . . Five . . . Six . . .'

Everyone was by now creasing up inside, yet not really knowing whether permitted to laugh or cry at the tragic comedy. Some actually doubled over, in an attitude of prayer, and laid their heads on the tables to try to conceal their unstoppable upsurge of mirth.

The healer cried to Sybil, 'STOP! STOP!' and decided he should try someone else. He jested as he asked her to sit down, 'You must have a prophetic spirit my dear.' Maybe he was trying to lighten the situation? Who can blame him?

As the meeting proceeded he bravely continued, 'There is someone with pains in the abdomen . . .'

Ever game, and now lip reading his dialect more effectively, Sybil was off her seat again; but this time hubby was hanging on firmly to her hand and thankfully she never made the front.

The next morning our man must have been severely shaken when he gave another of his special 'words' in the church meeting on a nearby housing estate. For there was Sybil again, this time with a pain in the knee and ready for prayer as always. You must commend her perseverance.

Sickness is not an easy subject to be jocular about, but I tell this story with confidence, for the great lady herself related it to me with such fun that tears of laughter rolled down my own face.

Where would we be if we could not laugh in life with all its tragedy?

Camphorated Oil

Back home in Canterbury, I remember my own first tentative steps into the realms of healing—several successes and a string of failures. One success I do recall because, looking back, it was so bizarre.

I had recently read a portion of scripture which exhorted the elders to anoint people with oil for healing, but I had no knowledge of how to do this.

Soon after I was called to a nearby house by a friend whose wife was ill in bed. I set off with a large bottle of camphorated oil and as much faith as I could muster. Once in the bedroom I poured the oil over the lady's head in the manner of anointing.

I had no idea the stuff came out so quickly.

In no time at all she was drenched and so was the bedding. The smell was incredibly pungent and I learned afterwards that it took days to go away. However, she was up and about in no time.

I hope it was more than the shock that moved her!

The Case of Aunt Emma

Almost the first healing experience in which I participated concerned a distant relative whom we called Aunt Emma. She was then well into her seventies. She lived some miles away in Faversham.

Motoring home for lunch one day I had a distinct impression I should call on my uncle and aunt. We did not know them well and had hardly ever visited. I tried hard to ignore the impression, but it persisted to the point of discomfort. So, following my instinct I turned the car round and drove about ten miles to their house.

When I arrived the elderly lady opened the door herself. She was doubled right over and on the point of tears. I asked her what on earth was the matter. She told me she had just come from the hospital, but they could not relieve her pain or straighten the back because that would cause complications to other treatment she was receiving at the time. She bemoaned the fact that she had planned to go with the church outing to Brighton, but now it was impossible. She was in such obvious agony.

Straight away my uncle whisked me into the garden and introduced me to a visiting university student who was pouring over his books in the summer sunshine. Uncle George then told him I was a great man of faith and if I had been alive years ago I would have been one of the prophets like Elijah or John the Baptist. I was totally amazed. I had no idea they even accepted my unusual calling, let alone revered it. The student showed evident scepticism and I could not blame him.

An inner 'still small voice' kept urging me to pray for

Auntie's healing, but I was plain scared and quite unprepared to act. This was all a new realm to me. However, I suddenly had an inspiration and asked if they had a Bible in the house. Being good Methodists of course they had. I turned to the Gospel of Mark and pointed out a passage which said that the disciples would lay hands on the sick and they would recover.

I then turned, faced Aunt Emma and gravely asked her if she felt I was a real disciple. 'Oh yes!' she said unhesitatingly.

'Then what will happen if I pray for you now?' I demanded forcibly to cover my feeling of inadequacy.

She stalled twice, groaning, amidst her great pain and still from the bent position, that she had heard of others getting help by divine healing. I gave her one last chance and repeated the question.

'Not others. What will happen to you?' I challenged again.

'I will recover!' she stated confidently.

Without thinking I clapped my hands on her back ready to pray, but before I could start she screamed out, 'Your hands are red hot!'

To my dismay, before my eyes her back began to straighten and it was obvious from her smiling face that all the pain had left.

Pandemonium broke out as Auntie began to run round and round the kitchen table shouting:

'I am going to Brighton! I am going to Brighton!'

The student stood stupefied. He grasped my hand and stated seriously:

'May I wish you the very best of luck in your ministry, sir!'

Uncle George was by now scribbling the name of his

newly ordained Church of England son on a piece of paper and urging me to visit him if ever I was on the South Coast.

However, I wanted out. I was totally devoid of faith and courage as I bolted up the garden path before Aunt Emma dropped dead from exhaustion. Throughout the furious drive home I dreaded that a phone call would await me with news of a relapse.

My fears were sustained all week long until the Saturday morning when Aunt Emma rang and told my wife that she had never felt fitter in her life.

Well, there is a turn-up for the book! Whose faith was it, I wonder?

Good God!

'A man does not believe what he would but what he can, and I cannot do Him so great a wrong as to suppose He will condemn His creatures for what is no fault of theirs.'
W. Somerset Maugham

'God is good, and all things which proceed from Him are good.'
Hildegard of Bingen

'How great is Thy goodness.'
David the Psalmist

Omnipresent Reading

I have often wondered what God does all day!

I picked up a few clues when on retreat in the delightful Highway Hotel which lies on the long steep hill that is Burford, renowned gateway to the gentle Cotswolds.

We had in our company a most cultured minister, who at one early-morning prayer session, cleared his throat and in his educated deliberate tones, addressed the Almighty thus:

'As You have no doubt already seen in *The Times* this morning, Lord . . .'

Well, I have always thought God was a gentleman.

Now I know He votes Conservative too . . .

I wonder if He solves the crossword and how long He takes?

O Ye of Little Faith

Despite being about the highest paid person in the local fellowship I gave up my secular employment to pursue what was known as a 'full time ministry' or 'living by faith'. (I thought it was the just who live by faith, not just the ministers?) My departure meant a severe blow to our tithed offerings and an even more severe test of my faith.

The elders gave their verbal but not financial confirmation, saying that if my calling was really of God then He would supply all my needs or cause others to do so. I secretly hoped that He would be benevolent and grant me a ministry of grace and not judgement. I could not see the saints cheerfully coughing up to support a wandering itinerant with an unpleasant message. Little did I know how unpopular the message of outrageous grace could be to those who wanted to earn their place in heaven or stack up Brownie points once tucked in the fold down here.

To make sure we did not spend more money than we needed I ensured that the central heating did not come on except during the very coldest of snaps. As a family of six we ate, were clothed and paid our mortgage, but so often at the eleventh hour.

Other travelling men seemed to do much better, in fact one of the more successful called on me one day and having observed our living standard remarked haughtily, 'Man, you are not living by faith, you are dying by faith!'

Well, the good book says, 'He gives to every man a measure of faith' and my measure seems pretty small—but I am still here.

A New Method of Faith

Recently a bank manager friend visited me and asked how I managed to sustain myself in evident comfort. For many years I had lived 'by faith' as we used to call it, I explained; that is waiting to see what turned up in the mail or by way of personal gifts. Now, I told him, I am aged sixty-six and have a basic social security pension plus whatever generous folk send me to put a little jam on the bread

'Do you have to solicit money?' he asked openly. I blinked and supposed bank managers were used to asking direct questions.

'Oh no,' I replied, 'that would not be faith at all.' But inwardly I had to admit to the odd hint when up against it. 'Eileen has always had more faith than me,' I continued, 'but that doesn't cause me any concern. Faith is a gift surely; you can't get it by straining. When I felt I had nothing to say then I went back to work. There were jobs in those days.'

'Glad to hear it,' the finance man said approvingly. 'I once had a a chap come to speak at our fellowship and after the first evening he took me aside and asked if I would like to support him on a regular basis.'

My face registered astonishment at the minister's audacity.

'What did you reply?' I asked tentatively.

'Just said No!' he replied without batting an eye. 'I am used to turning down requests for money!'

Nice one, I thought. And smiled to myself all day.

Many times I have pondered the legitimacy of leaders who constantly exhort people to give money, or teach that their followers ought to exercise faith in financial matters, yet themselves live off the regular tithes of others. I can't make it all add up. It's not for me anyway.

Your Money or Your Life

'If you send a donation then I will ascend into my prayer tower and offer a prayer on your behalf,' said the British mailshot from an American TV evangelist. The same man also later informed his audience that unless they subscribed several million dollars by a certain date, God was going to take his life.

How gullible are we supposed to be?

Anyway my friend John West tucked away in Essex was not in the mood to respond to his junk mail. However, he is not an ungenerous man, so he wrote and told Mr Roberts that if *he* would send over some money then John would ascend into his tower and offer his prayers.

Snap!

I thought that was neat.

But I must confess to being rather shaken when I was visiting Wisconsin near the close of the eighties. Young people everywhere were wearing T-shirts with large capitals L-O-R-D emblazoned across the chest.

'Lord Who?' I enquired.

'Oh no,' they replied with a wide grin, 'it stands for Let Oral Roberts Die!'

A bit cruel. But you could say he asked for it.

Ministry of Funny Walks

It was over thirty years ago that a small procession of elders emerged from the broom cupboard that was our prayer room in a Nissen hut-type building located at the seaside town of Deal in Kent.

I was next to last out as I was to be the speaker on this particular Sunday morning. As we slowly made our way to the platform the senior pastor behind me whispered in his broad Irish brogue:

'Have you hurt your leg, Brother Smith?'

'No. There is nothing wrong with my leg,' I whispered back.

'Oh. It must just be your spiritual walk then,' he smiled.

I have never forgotten the gentle admonition.

Well-meaning gentlemen seemed at pains to whisper advice to me in those early days.

On a somewhat longer walk, I remember trudging the Deal seafront early one Sunday morning, desperately trying to get some inspiration for the ministry I was due to utter in a few hour's time.

Surprised by a gentle tap on my shoulder, I turned to see a pair of twinkling eyes and a nodding head. They were possessed by the oldest member of the congregation, already in his eighties. 'Old Brother Holloway' we called him, or OBH for short. He was a constant source of encouragement to me in those early days.

On this occasion he put his mouth close to my ear and whispered:

'It is perfectly safe to trust the Lord, old boy.'

He had obviously sussed out my worrying frame of mind.

It is taking a long, long time to find out that he was right.

Getting Married in the Morning

It's always surprising to me that we never seem content with people where they are. We always want to change them. Lovers, for instance, fall in love with someone whose personality attracts them and then set about a lifetime of trying to alter them. Church leaders—ah, but that's another story!

This tendency was beautifully illustrated to me some years ago on the way to a wedding programmed to take place around midday. I am very punctilious and hate being late for anything—and we were!

After emerging from the Blackwall Tunnel, north of the Thames, we got lost somewhere along the Mile End Road. Steam was beginning to rise from under my collar when I spotted two old fellas standing around outside a betting shop.

'Could you direct me to Southgate?' I asked politely.

Southgate being my ultimate destination and some miles north of London, I could see no problem. They did not even bother to confer but shook their heads in mournful unison.

'Archway?' (somewhat nearer) I asked, struggling manfully to suppress my irritation.

'Never 'eard of it, mate,' replied the surlier of the two in an extremely unhelpful tone.

'Finsbury Park. Arsenal. The Gunners!'

I was desperate now and grasping at any landmark *en route*, for I could almost hear the Wedding March. This mention of the local football team at last produced some animation. They conferred in urgent undertones for some time, as I grew more and more agitated. At last the grave interpreter returned.

'Sorry, mate,' he said with finality, 'you can't get there from 'ere!'

Well, I have many times thanked our Heavenly Host that we can get there from here, for unless He meets us where we are and takes us as we are, we'll never make that last great Wedding Feast at all.

A Slight Knock

I left home with no money. After a disastrous journey to Poole, to which destination I erroneously believed I would be divinely transported in time for an evening meeting, I returned to the church and gave a talk based on my many, many miles of weary foot-slogging.

'The Lord regardeth the legs of a man,' was my text, conveniently borrowed from the book of Psalms.

A sympathetic visitor from the nearby town of Deal heard my dissertation, no doubt took pity, and afterwards approached me and said he wanted to give me his car.

I was ecstatic. Wheels!

Perhaps the walk was not so entirely disastrous after all?

He went on to state, 'We have just bought a new one and didn't know what to do with our old Wolseley—it's rather ancient.'

He further informed me that there was a slight knock in the engine, but if nursed and not driven above 50 miles per hour he was sure it would last for ever. He eulogised about the engineering.

I heard: 'Old one . . . slight knock . . . rather ancient . . .'

Oh, I see!

The gift turned out to be immense black limousine which never failed to draw the eye.

Around that time I was travelling regularly with a friend (because JC sent them out 'by two and by two'!) and he would sit passively in the front alongside me, holding on to the hanging tassel, making me look like the chauffeur. His name was Ted and our family immediately nicknamed him 'Sir Edward'.

We three—the Wolseley, Sir Edward and me were to experience great things together before her final demise. Perhaps the finale was the most impressive, but that's another story.

Meanwhile we were glad to be mobile, even if conspicuous.

The Disrespect of Youth

I could never really afford good cars. A well-known friend of mine from South Chard in Somerset seemed to have much more faith and went for better models. He was sporting a brand new Jaguar while I was struggling along in the huge ancient Wolseley, reminiscent of the Keystone Cops with those huge sweeping mudguards—no wings in those days—which always afforded an excellent slide for any children in the vicinity of the parked monster.

Once as I drew near to the main roundabout in Canterbury I observed a group of a dozen boys seated in the centre, glaring in disbelief at my sedate approach. They were bedecked in the boaters and bow ties of The King's School. Each member of England's oldest public school was equipped with a pencil and paper and took notes of passing vehicles. As I passed they rose slowly as one body and raised their hats in mock deference.

I drove on blushing furiously and wondering who had given the sniggering word of command.

Back to my South Chard friend and his Jaguar who had so grandiosely come to town to speak at our small meeting.

Once he had delivered his oration we both had to attend a local house meeting to address a group of young people. Looking around I saw there were six teenage girls all needing a lift.

'Right, all pile in!' I shouted as we both stood holding our car doors open.

All six clambered into Harry's splendid automobile and left me to follow on alone. 'He not only has a new car, but he is also better looking!' I admitted with a self-centred sigh.

I do not remember whether I was solaced, blessed or patronised when he later left for home, and smiling as ever stated, 'Don't worry, Maurice, if God can give you the worst He can give you the best.'

I am not really sure to this day what he meant; but I think about it.

Knock, Knock

We were driving back from Bristol in our huge automobile, reflecting upon its sterling performance after several months of service at speeds far in excess of the advised fifty miles per hour, when I heard the ominous knock.

I have never been mechanically minded, which revealed itself in my prompt decision to put my toe down hard and get home as soon as possible.

As I pushed the speedo up to 70 the knocking got louder and louder. We went through Boughton village only five miles from home now and the noise was so loud that people came out of the shops to see what was happening.

The monster gamely faced the long 1 in 6 hill that led out of the village and which preceded the downhill run to the cathedral city.

As we ascended with pistons banging out their painful objection, I saw great clouds of smoke begin to fill the vehicle. However it was no time to stop so near to home, so I opened the windows, waved my hands in front of my face to clear a view and pressed on, in spite of the now absolutely deafening noise coming from under the bonnet.

Well she reached the summit all right. But just opposite a dilapidated garage on the brow the beast decided enough was enough. With one almighty explosion bits if metal flew all over the road and we came to a grinding halt totally enveloped in smoke.

I climbed out dejectedly to face a grimy mechanic who ambled across the road, lifted the bonnet without a word, saw the gaping hole in the engine cover and stated baldly, 'Finished, mate, I'm afraid.'

'Oh!'

'I'll shove it on my scrap heap and hire you a taxi if you like.'

And that was it.

So much for good intentions of taking it steady and lasting for ever.

When I arrived home my two youngest boys had their noses pressed to the first-floor window as ever, awaiting my return. They nearly burst into tears when the story was told, for they loved that old car. Never again would they be able to travel along with the sliding roof open and stand on the seat with their heads protruding. No more, thanks to Dad.

'Another of your little jobs!' they moaned.

That has become a family motto. If we ever start our own company (heaven forbid!) it will be known as 'A. L. J. Limited'—another little job.

Well, you can't be good at all things, can you?

The Blue Mini

The family went without a car for some time and one night at bedtime our youngest son said, 'Why can't we have a car like other families?'

I told him I had not got the money. I was serving God!

'Why don't you pray for one?' he asked promptly.

I informed him that if he had some faith then he should pray, not me.

We knelt by the bed and the five-year-old said confidently, 'Dear God, please send Daddy a blue Mini . . . Thank you.'

I must admit I rather wished he had been more ambitious, but anyway I knew God wouldn't listen to the small details.

At the end of that week I went by train to Reading to address a house meeting. After it was over a young man called across the room, 'How did you get here tonight, Maurice?'

I explained that I had come up to London and then changed trains down to Reading.

'Here!' he said, throwing some keys across the room. 'You can have my car, your need is greater than mine.'

I stammered out a mixture of objections and thanks, but he insisted.

'You'll find it parked at the end of the road,' he replied, 'You can't miss it, it's the blue Mini.'

I was absolutely flabbergasted. No less.

When I drove round the roundabout alongside my home the next day, the two young faces were there beaming down at me as though it was all the most natural thing in the world. There was no element of surprise.

Must be something to this 'babes and sucklings' business.

Wish I could work it!

More Haste Less Speed

The resplendent commissionaire was not impressed when I clobbered a concrete post coming out of a Park Lane hotel where I had been wined and dined by an admirer of my modest speaking talents.

A fine start to the week I thought, as I phoned my insurance broker.

'No, there was no one else involved . . . I was in a hurry . . . OK, I do understand it will affect my no-claims bonus!'

Later the same week I drove on to a petrol station forecourt, noticing as I did so that there were no cars waiting in line for a car wash. I purchased my token and drove round to gain immediate entry. By this time there were two cars in front of me whose owners had parked first and then gone for the token.

I was in no particular hurry but felt irritated by this petty unfairness. The owners took ages to emerge from the forecourt shop and I made a move to get out and remonstrate with them. A little voice inside me whispered, 'Leave it alone, Maurice. Relax.'

Still no one arrived. Leaving my Rover 2000 Automatic ticking over in neutral I started to climb out. It seemed as though I had to break through a kind of peace barrier inside me as I huffed and puffed away. Didn't someone say, 'Let the peace of God rule (umpire) in your hearts'? The umpire was calling a foul on this occasion but I kept on playing.

'What on earth is your driver playing at?' I demanded of the stout lady occupying the passenger seat of the car in front.

'I beg your pardon . . . ?' she sniffed.

But I was no longer listening.

My car must have somehow shuddered into reverse for I caught sight of it gliding across the tarmac towards a ten-foot white fence.

I chased it to no avail. It crashed right through the fence and came to rest framed in white against the tyre of a huge lorry parked on the adjacent property.

'Anyone hurt, sir?' politely enquired the Jeevish attendant when I reported the accident.

'No' I replied sheepishly. 'There was actually no one in the car at the time.'

Off to phone the broker again. ' . . . there was nobody else involved . . . I was in a hurry . . . (I lied) . . . yes, I understand about the bonus.'

Now I drive round to the car wash first and get my token afterwards.

But I do wish I had listened to that still small voice the first time.

Amazing Graces

Some of the most insincere prayer seems to be invoked by the habit of 'saying grace' before meals. I am immediately reminded of Peter Marshall's comment on being faced with a post-Thanksgiving dinner, when he said to his wife, 'Darling, you say grace; the Lord knows I can't stand turkey hash!'

I've heard some shockers myself. How about the wealthy lady who, in a highpitched nasal voice, called down the blessing of the Divine Provider in rhyme? The last two lines of which ran:

'. . . And as the sugar dissolves in the tea,
So may our lives be lost in Thee.'

A not-so-refined rendition came from the burly leader of a young people's camp who shouted:

'Rubadub dub
Thanks for the grub!'

Introducing the raucous, how about the single bellowed pentecostal 'Hallelujah!', which caused the convener of the meeting to turn and ask if someone else would like to say grace properly?

The next incident must have been repeated often. One of a pair of young enthusiastic twins gave endless thanks for every member of the family, every tribe and every nation, until the food was stone cold and quite unpalatable. Everyone was far too religious to suggest enough was enough!

On the other hand, my favourite snub to the religious came when a friend of mine in his nineties, and still travelling in ministry, was asked before the meal by a Bishop, 'Norman, will you pray?'

'Certainly,' he responded with supreme innocence. 'What about?'

I can never quite tell with him. He is a regular twinkler and they always have me foxed. I sometimes wonder if that wily atheist Aldous Huxley didn't have it right when he caused one of his characters to say, 'In Pala, we don't say grace before meals. We say it with meals. Or rather we don't say grace; we chew it.'

'Chew it?'

'Grace is the first mouthful of each course chewed and chewed until there is nothing left of it. And all the time you are chewing you pay attention to the flavour of the food, to its consistency and temperature, to the pressures on your teeth and the feel of the muscles in your jaw.'

True savouring, I suppose, is the epitome of grace.

Checked Out

It was the first time Nick was ever invited to travel away and address a gathering of people. To middle-class Camberley in Surrey he went.

Of course he knew it was customary for the leader to approach you afterwards with a sealed envelope, inside which was the 'ministry gift'. Either that or some notes screwed up so small you literally needed to iron them out before they were presentable. We had funny ways.

On this occasion the leader broke the mould and gave him the envelope before he spoke, saying he did not want to forget it. Nick hoped they liked what he had to say.

Our aspiring itinerant could not wait to see how much he had got. Within two minutes of receiving the gift he was in the lavatory ripping open the envelope.

He was amazed to see the cheque made out to a Mrs Somebody or other. Obviously the cheque had got into the wrong envelope.

Well, he would play it cool and keep the gift until after the meeting and then tell the leader. That way it would not look as if he was desperate for the money.

No such luck!

As he came out of the toilet the leader was there waiting and walked into the lounge with him.

'There has been a mistake,' the leader began apologetically. 'We got the envelopes mixed. Could we have yours back? It seems my wife wrote a cheque for our aunt and . . .'

Nick didn't catch the rest. He was contemplating the sinking feeling in the pit of his stomach.

Of course he said he was sorry. But it was a dreadful moment. Only two minutes after receipt and he had to produce an already-opened envelope.

The room had gone strangely quiet—you know the experience. It was obvious to all why he had so urgently answered the call of nature.

The Camberley leader smiled ruefully.

Thankfully maturity prevailed and both parties had a good laugh.

'Be sure your sins will find you out!'

First Steps of Faith

Aaron, a travelling minister still in his early days, was asked to speak at a northern University. He travelled up from the southwest by train and used up all his money except for five shillings (25p today).

Unfortunately and unusually, he was given no gift after the ministry, but he was determined not to beg (or perhaps not to 'let his left hand know what his right hand was doing!').

Slowly and thoughtfully he made his way to the railway station, but was inwardly dismayed that he was not able to shake off a following of appreciative students.

He was rehearsing to himself how Hudson Taylor, a renowned man of faith, had in similar circumstances at Shanghai Station got into the queue in perfect peace, assured that God would provide his fare. He had seen a literal miracle, for an unknown man in front of him had unexpectedly turned and said, 'I'll pay this gentleman's fare.' Not a previous word was spoken between them. Or so the story goes.

Our budding man of God decided to follow the precedent and stoically got in the queue and started to edge forward, whilst the bevvy of admiring students were still in earshot attendance.

Finally he arrived at the ticket window but no miracle had taken place.

'Yes? Where to?' enquired the booking clerk.

In desperation, and in the quietest voice possible, Aaron whispered, 'How far can I go for five shillings?'

A bit of comedown, but a good try!

He purchased a ticket for a short ride down the line

and hurried through the barrier.

Divine providence had not entirely deserted him however, for on his necessarily short journey a ticket inspector came through the train and, learning of his predicament, said that on proof of identity they could bill him the rest of the fare to his home address.

Not exactly a miracle, but useful.

Any Expenses?

I guess students are often genuinely hard up.

It was the end of another weekend at Keele University, in Staffordshire. Again two of us had been invited. This time a different minister came with me. The look-em-in-the-eye straightforward Dave.

It was a time of considerable spiritual uplift and as we prepared to leave for our community home some hundreds of miles south on the outskirts of London, the Christian Union leader shyly asked us, 'Do you have any expenses?'

I was trying to think of a suitable answer that would be honest but inoffensive, when I heard my colleague say, 'Yes, a wife and two children!'

The young man took the point.

More University Tests

My colleague and I were relieved to finally arrive at London University for a weekend of meetings, relieved because we had made it without running out of petrol. We had driven up from the Kent coast, once again without a penny between us and the petrol gauge firmly glued on empty.

All through the weekend the young leader kept approaching me and whispering that he must give us something to cover our expenses.

Finally, as we were walking along the London pavement he said it again. I opened the car door, sat in and wound down the window expectantly.

He leaned his head down and asked, 'Would ten shillings cover it?'

I told him no, that would not even cover the petrol. He said, with obvious reluctance, that he would make it a pound.

I sat there waiting, dreading starting up in case there was insufficient petrol to motivate the engine.

He finally leaned down again, put his head through the window and said, 'We'll be sending it to you.'

Well thanks!

The car did start and we pulled slowly out into the traffic ready to head south for as far as we could. Suddenly a young man started waving frantically, so we stopped. He asked if we could possibly take him and his wife to the Mill Hill area. The lady in question stood meekly by his side, being very evidently about ten months pregnant.

Now Mill Hill was about ten miles north of London.

'Certainly,' said Ted, my co-minister, promptly moving from the front passenger seat to help them in.

'He's done it again!' I realised and sweated every mile in the wrong direction fearing we were going to chug to a halt. Ted had a reputation for this sort of thing, having once ended up sleeping on Charing Cross station and coming home on the milk train!

The man told us they were missionaries home on furlough from the Red Sea so that his wife could have the child. We talked endlessly about the Charismatic Movement now sweeping the churches and apparently what we said encouraged them greatly, for by the time we arrived they were both visibly excited.

We shook hands on the pavement in Mill Hill and as I did so I found a five-pound note pressed in my hand. We had said nothing, but we were extremely grateful and headed straight for the nearest petrol station.

Maybe God does move in mysterious ways?

A Filling Station

We were just a couple of greenhorns, but our host for the weekend was himself an itinerant of some experience. Previously he had been a local businessman and a JP of considerable renown. As we left Edgar's house in Plymouth he was standing waving on the pavement.

Suddenly he dashed to the kerb with one of his seeming flashes of inspiration and said we were to follow him out of town or we might get lost, then he'd return home.

As we reached the outskirts he drove into a petrol station and we followed him to wait. I sat impatiently thinking that this was rubbing our problem in a bit, as our petrol tank was registering the usual position and we were once again broke and unable to rectify matters.

After he had filled up he waved us to the pump and cheerfully called to the attendant:

'Fill these lads up too!'

He stood by as the dial hand on the old-fashioned pump went whirling round and round in circles. We had the old Wolseley with the large tank and had been bone dry.

Edgar's face was a picture as he watched the dial.

'My, you fellas were low!' he said with a knowing smile and went off to the pay booth. Had somebody upstairs been telling on us or what?

The Tale of Two Fivers

The same bright pair of new boys were leaving Torbay Court, a hotel on the south Devon coast where we had attended a conference. The situation was normal—no money between us but we still had plenty of Edgar's petrol swishing happily around in our tank.

As I said my goodbyes, the hotel owner generously gave me a fiver to help us on our long journey across to Kent.

We never revealed our needs, but everyone knew we had no jobs and had families at home, so some folk gave us gifts to help out and promote the message. A fiver was often the going rate in those days and sometimes we ministers helped each other along. I recall at one period I learned that the same five-pound note was passed on by post through three or four of us, finally ending up where it started. We all declared our incomes, so I guess the only real beneficiary was the Inland Revenue.

I told Ted I had the gift and he replied that he also had been given five pounds. While we each went to pack our bags I decided this was a bonanza and I would put my fiver in the giftbox by the door, for the whole enterprise was run on a semifaith basis.

Some miles down the road we pulled into a layby to eat our sandwiches and I told Ted what I had done.

He smiled his usual wry smile and confided, 'So did I, Maurice!'

We were back to square one again.

Situation normal.

Manna From Heaven

I really don't know why I have always been so bad at trusting for provision, for I have had encouragement enough goodness knows.

There was the sunny day I was meandering along Castle Steet in Canterbury, soon after giving up my well-paid job and starting on the road as a travelling minister. I was entirely without stipend or any guarantee of provision except I felt sure that I was called to do what I was doing.

Madness some called it.

I stopped to look up at the brave ruins of the Norman Castle and as I did so I had a little moan at the Almighty, saying I was finding it so difficult to be at peace not knowing where my next meal was coming from.

It was not so much for myself as for my wife and four children. I think.

As I stood looking up in the air I found myself mumbling away, 'It was OK for Elijah. When he was in need the ravens fed him!'

Just then a blackbird flew out of the castle and circled about twenty feet above my head.

I was astounded to see a large piece of bread in its beak.

As I watched it dropped the bread right down at my feet.

Well, I've never wanted through all the years, but it has looked pretty close at times.

'O ye of little faith!'

Professional Itinerants?

Dave and I were always on the move. One night stands were our speciality. One would talk and the other sing—it was kind of double act, not your normal ministry by any means. Never quite knew where we would sleep and often had sleeping bags ready in the boot of the car.

One night early in our travelling relationship we were shown into a small single room. There was one single bed and as the elder of the two I was granted the privilege.

'By the way,' I said as we tucked down, 'I snore quite loud I am told.'

My compatriot said he did not mind and lay squashed on the floor between the wall and my bed. We were both soon well away, for it had been a very late night.

All through the small hours I kept being awakened by his flailing arms. I have never known anything like it. At one time I thought he was having fits in the night.

At breakfast I was bleary-eyed and not in the sweetest of tempers.

'I warned you about my snoring,' I complained, 'but do you know you thrash your arms about? You hit me several times and woke me up!'

'I know, I was trying to stop you snoring!' he replied.

Oh!

Anyway, we went on travelling happily together, but thankfully not often sleeping in the same room.

I'm still sure I don't snore very loud really.

Well I've never heard it.

Lost, Stolen or Strayed?

This is one of those stories I cannot resist, although its connection with overtly spiritual matters is tenuous to say the least. Perhaps the nearest I can get is tenuous alignment with not letting your left hand know what your right is doing!

On the one hand the ambitious plan was to obtain a good sales position with the 3M Company from the US of A, whose offices were in the Strand. On the other hand the deeper ploy was to decide I did not want it and introduce a less qualified friend who was conveniently waiting downstairs. Needless to say it did not quite come off.

The vehicle around which the incident revolved was a brand new 1954 new-shape Ford Prefect supplied by my current company. I was living in the Cotswolds and visited the Strand way down in London during working hours. (This begins to look as if a more suitable text would again have been 'Be sure your sins will find you out.')

The weather was wet and blustery as I parked in a side street leading down to the Thames Embankment. After the interview I walked along the Strand and looked down the side street to find the car was gone.

Very reluctantly I trudged to Covent Garden police station to report the loss and arrived there soaked through. The sergeant at the desk was a very intolerant man and he'd had a bad day before I arrived.

No, I did not know the registration number! The car was new and I had not yet memorised it.

This did not help the man at all. With a 'Calling all

cars' system which I had only seen in the cinema, he reluctantly put out an alert to the London area with a vehicle description but no registration number. He then dismissed me saying they would let me know if it was found, which in the circumstances was most unlikely.

As I slouched sadly to the Underground station I glanced down a side street off the Strand and there was my fawn Ford Prefect.

I quickly realised I had previously looked down the wrong street.

Fearing a verbal assault from the sergeant I half-decided to get in and drive off, but a deeper fear of being caught stealing my own vehicle was enough to deter that thought. So it was back to the police station.

'Now what do you want? Have you remembered the number?'

'Er . . . no,' I mumbled into my coat collar, 'I've . . . found the car!'

Well, the man nearly went beserk. He put out another 'Calling all cars' and returned to give me a thorough roasting for wasting police time.

You decide on the text. If you think it deserves one. I like the story.

Diary of a Fast

In the early days of my travelling ministry I decided I needed a jolly good fast. It was not exactly God-inspired, rather motivated by the fact that all the big men said they did it and got great results. To you it probably sounds like a recipe for disaster and you are not far wrong.

Sunday evening I dramatically stated, 'Eileen, I want nothing else to eat until next Sunday when I am due to speak at Cambridge University.' Having left school at the ripe old age of fourteen years I was naturally terrified at performing before all these young hyper-intellectuals.

Well, things started to go wrong right from the start. During the Monday I developed severe pains in the kidney area which persisted right down the groin to the tender nether regions. Hour by hour the pain increased, but I steadfastly refused medical help, insisting I was in God's hands and He knew what He was doing. It was a kind of spiritual whistling in the dark I suppose.

Day 2 was to bring no improvement either. I had no telephone at the time and a friend and neighbour took all my calls. When I was feeling at my lowest he popped his head round the bedroom door and informed me: 'We've just had a call from a member of a Black Magic circle, they say they have secured your life. They say you will not live.' Well thanks!

I was lying there in bed, grey as an old army blanket and pondering this unexpected good news when another close friend looked in to see how I was progressing. He took one look at me and involuntarily exclaimed, 'My word, you do look terrible!' Thanks again.

Day 3 and I could cope with no more. I've always

had a low pain threshold. So I got up, dressed slowly and trudged the streets of Canterbury, doing my best to converse with the Almighty. The word 'stones' kept popping into my mind and so I tried desperately to con - sider 'Living stones', 'Temple stones' and every other type of stone I thought the Divine Builder would be likely to be interested in. Eventually the thought proved to be truly prophetic and very much down to earth. Meanwhile it was a painful trudge I can tell you that, as I resolutely passed through my doctor's surgery door and the entrance to the Kent and Canterbury Hospital, holding to my spiritual fast.

On returning home I ripped my clothes off in a foul temper. I remember the shirt buttons shooting across the room like machine-gun bullets. Then I swore for the first time since my black-to-white conversion many years previously and told God to stick His 'on high call- ing' on the wall. I'd given up a good job, a high salary, and was now living on a relative pittance to support my wife and four children. Now when I had decided on this major fast to become a mighty spiritual warrior, all He could come up with was a good dose of agony. Other 'great men of God' had relayed to me the fruits of their fastings: their great revelations, increased power, or a new sense of direction; but as for me, the best I could offer was a few kidney stones.

Back in bed I pondered the great Cedars of Lebanon which the Israelites had cut down to build the Temple and realised that I had felt rather like one of those important pillars. Now, after all the years of being cut down, shaped and planed, there was a knot in the wood (I had sworn and told him to poke my calling!) and it seemed I was a reject.

Eileen stood by during this the first of many of my spiritual fiascos, despairing that I would ever recover and be the man I longed to be.

I ate nothing all week and just before midnight on the Saturday, after a blurred six days and nights in bed, I looked up at the ceiling and murmured despondently, 'Well, that's it! I can't go to Cambridge tomorrow in this state . . . or ever speak again. I'll just have to ask someone else. I am too weak and besides . . . I am a complete failure . . .'

It really did seem like the end of my world to me.

I remained very still. Then I noticed that the silence was strangely intense, so that you could almost reach out and touch it. I felt as though an important moment had arrived, but then I am always dramatic!

I was surprised as a still voice deep inside me whispered some words I will never forget.

'You've . . . discovered My hobby . . . Maurice.'

'Eh? What?'

'I collect failures, son. I only collect failures.'

Oh I see!

It was then I strangely knew that if I told the pain to go, it would. Don't ask me how I knew; I just knew. So that's what I did. Not a shout, but a whisper. Not a mighty, 'In the Name of Jesus!' But just one quiet word: 'Go!' And the pain left instantly. It was midnight and the raver was turned back to reason again.

Of course I went to Cambridge. But in absolute total weakness. A grateful Collected Failure. I don't think I have ever spoken more effectively in my life. But then we mustn't start measuring, must we?

What a fast! Looking back, it was so worthwhile. But I won't try again.

Seconds Out!

I had always been bullied by other 'big leaders' in spite of all my years in ministry and being recognised as a prophet to the movement. Attempting to sell my car proved no exception.

'You have accepted too little for it,' exclaimed the apostle.

'But I am no good at this bargaining business and anyway, the buyer is one of the fellowship. I feel happy about it.'

'You are wasting money. You should advertise and see what response you get.'

Well, I tried to resist, but with no avail. This man just did not realise how strong his opinions were and how everyone felt obliged to buckle under and do what he wanted. So the advert went in the local paper.

The phone rang and a Jewish voice muffled by a dreadfully heavy cold suggested I take the car round to his house as he was too unwell to get out. I made it clear I was not prepared to barter, the price was the price; after all I was only asking a little more than offered by our Christian car dealer. I had a bad feeling about the deal even then, but reluctantly agreed to drive over. Anything appeared better than arguing it all out again with the ultrapositive spiritual leader of the flock.

I climbed the stairs to the top flat in an expensive block and rang the bell. As I did so I thought I recognised the unusual name printed on the plate alongside. The possible buyer had his hat and coat already on, ready to test drive, and began complaining about having to go out on such a cold day, as if his cold was all my fault.

He clapped eyes on the vehicle and exclaimed immediately: 'Well, it is not in the condition which you described in the paper, is it?'

Here we go!

When we got back to the flat he started to point to massive cups and shields adorning the place. 'My son is a black belt Judo fighter,' he said. 'Did you recognise my name on the bell?' I said it was familiar.

'I was the lightweight boxing champion of the world!' he stated. I remembered then that he'd taken the title from Jimmy Wilde years before.

'Now back to business,' he barked through a germ-filled handkerchief and made me some ridiculous offer. I got up to leave saying I had made it clear I was not going to discuss the price.

'Get the money from under the mattress,' he shouted at his wife, 'and hurry up. I am feeling tired already.' She gave a despairing look and left the room.

Eventually, after he had continually waved the large sheaf of notes before my eyes, I agreed to take just twenty-five pounds more than my previous offer. Whereupon he picked up the car key, thrust the money into my hands and began to usher me out. I resisted the haste and sat down to count the money while he kept up a nonstop bombardment of words telling me how ill he felt and how I had wasted his whole afternoon when he could have been in bed. My head was in a whirl.

'There is one hundred pounds short . . .' I nervously declared, having counted over and over again amid the confusion. He retorted that it was all there when he gave it to me and was I suggesting he was trying to swindle me? I told him he could search my pockets if he wanted to, for I had not got the money. He stood up, glowered down at me and spat out, 'The money was all there when I gave it to you. That's it!'

I glanced around the array of trophies, over to his wife's pitying eyes—she had obviously been all through this before—and then up into the threatening blood-shot orbs. I was sorely tempted to take what I had and escape in one piece.

'N-no . . .' I said with a stammer, 'We will call the police from here. I will not leave the room. They can search me if you won't.'

How I held out I don't know. It took a long time, but I did. Eventually he swore at his wife and told her to get another hundred pounds. He then rammed the extra notes into my hands and told me he had lost a lot of money on the deal. He then reluctantly offered to run me home in spite of his dreadful snuffling. Finally he shook my hand as I got out of the car, which seemed an inexplicable gesture after all the insults.

When I shakily arrived indoors I saw that Mike the police sergeant from across the road was there chatting to my wife. When I poured out the story he told me I had been very fortunate—many people would have been intimidated into leaving without the balance of the money.

After a few minutes the phone rang. It was the man himself . . . already! 'I have rung up to . . . apologise' he oozed amid the coughing and spluttering. 'It was that bloody woman. After you'd gone she found a hundred pounds on the floor by the bed.' I explained to the sergeant saying we must have misjudged the man. 'Not a bit of it old son' he replied sagely, 'That is his way of preventing you reporting to the police. An old ruse!'

When I told my dealer friend about the incident he

smiled knowingly while confiding, 'I am afraid your tough guy is well known in the trade, Maurice.' Once again I realised I should have listened to that small inner voice and not been harassed by the strong views of others. I felt worn out, and all for twenty-five pounds!

I purposed (once again) to start living my own way and not to let folk press their lifestyle on me. However it was quite a while before I shook completely free and was able to tell the big men that I was their equal, before I could look them in the eye and say, ' I will run my life my own way. You should be teaching people to be themselves, not to copy you'.

I thank God that day did come, but the top brass did not like it.

Huge Roastie

A group of eminent ministering Brethren had met for a day of fellowship, prayer and to seek the Lord (He was lost?) for a prophetic overview of His work in the nation. This was obviously very big-time. The meeting was held at the home of the Most Eminent of all who had a pleasantly large house in the West Country.

As the brothers travailed in prayer their meditations were disturbed by the sweet savour of the dinner being prepared for them. It smelled so delicious that the assembled prophets did not need bidding twice to come to the table. Roast beef, Yorkshire pudding, more vegetables than you could begin to count, and finally a huge dish of gorgeous crispy roast potatoes was set forth.

Just as they were about to make a start the telephone rang and the host left the table to take the call in the next room.

'Hope he's not too long,' said one brother speaking for them all 'It'll get cold'—whereupon he reached out and took a piping hot 'roastie' from the dish and after blowing on it between his fingers, deftly popped the appetiser into his mouth. All this to the shock, secret admiration and perhaps even envy of the rest.

Shortly the host returned to his place at the head of the table, and turning to the man of great liberty said, 'Perhaps you would say grace for us, brother?' As if they hadn't waited long enough!

However, the assembled company of leaders duly bowed their heads and closed their eyes in expectation. 'For what we are about to receive . . .' began Brother X, still with a suspicion of something in his mouth, 'and for the roast potato which I have already received, may the Lord make us truly thankful.'

A twinkle was detected in most of the opening eyes; but the eminent host was not amused.

'Perhaps you would say it again for us properly?' he suggested coldly.

The splendid dinner wasn't very warm by now either.

Not to the Naturally Wise . . .

Of course there was a time when I knew exactly in what manner and under what condition He would come. But not any more.

As I keep repeating, I know less and less, but feel more and more secure in that. God now seems so big, His purposes so vast, that to comprehend Him seems a bit presumptuous. I was a very spiritual cleverdick at one time, but now thankfully those days are gone. A good dose of sorrow, pain, failure and loss, plus all the other things that triumphalistic Christians have said I should have avoided with a lot more faith, have seen to that.

A friend of ours of whom I am very fond is well known for getting angry. It is something I like about her for you always know just where you are. Recently she heard that I had been offered a job in Galilee and was obviously intrigued.

'Has this got something to do with the Second Coming?' she demanded.

'Oh no,' I replied. 'I am not well up on subjects like that.'

Upon further questioning I said I knew in my head what the New Testament said in various places, but in my heart I really had no idea whether Jesus was going to come feet first or head first, whether He would zoom in from a million feet and land spot on the Mount of Olives, or if He was going to appear in His people. However I had a sense of excitement.

'I just don't know any more,' I concluded with a smile.

The lady's eyes flashed at their best as she flung out:

'No! You may not, Maurice, but it would be just like you to be there if He did come!'

I felt a rosy glow inside and just a little complimented. Now that would be nice, I thought; for when He came the first time all the experts got it wrong and missed Him and I felt quietly convinced that it would be the same the next time around. It took a wisdom not of this world to locate Him. It always does.

I'd rather keep looking and hoping, not knowing much, but still with a burning heart. I have found that too much information takes the mystery out of the love affair and that would ruin it all for me.

I hope my dear angry friend is right.

Where Are We Going?

This story has no right to be here. However, I like it.

It is not directly related to 'Christian' things. But as I never tire of saying, we can't really separate life into sacred and secular, can we? Not if we are going to be wholesome.

The yarn concerns my youngest son, who has always been a bit of a card.

He had just commenced working as a steward aboard the Folkestone to Boulogne ferry. The crew went back and forth twice in one day with hardly time to draw a breath between collecting crocks, washing up, cleaning down and a thousand and one other jobs.

He relates how one frightfully well-spoken lady apprehended him in the midst of his hectic menial tasks and demanded, 'Steward! When do we dock?'

She was apparently astounded by his genuine but unhelpful reply:

'Madam, I don't even know which way we are going!'

My son and I would admit that we don't always know which way we are going, but we are most certainly glad that God does. See, I wiggled Him in there at the end!

A Broken Window

Of course sometimes things do actually go.

Whilst living in a community in Chigwell, David came to me wreathed in smiles to relate a family story.

He had heard his son pacing up and down outside his study door for ages. Eventually the lad burst in looking very crestfallen and his father asked him what was the matter.

The boy explained that about an hour before he had broken a window in the conservatory. It had obviously been a long hour before he had plucked up the courage to tell his Dad.

'It's all right son, I know,' said David.

'How do you know, Dad?' the boy asked with wide eyes.

'I heard it go!' was the smiling reply.

I sometimes think it is like that with us and God.

He knows. He hears it go.

Why do we waste so long fretting over things?

Best just to get it off our chests.

I'm Driving in the Rain

I had always been a fairweather Christian and never liked a wet grey day. At the time in question my wife and I had opted for a weekend Bargain Break in the Peak District to celebrate our wedding anniversary. Do understand we are talking twenty years ago when I was a mere spiritual infant.

It was one of those lean periods when I possessed no car, but a friend generously offered to lend me his MG Sports which was very low-slung and a desperate struggle to get down into. More importantly it had windows which did not fit all that well.

As though by design the weather forecast was gloomy.

Another friend, who was a fine graphic designer, had long been bombarding us with a stream of virtues concerning integrity in the realms of colour, shade and texture. He loved all that nature had to teach us and once gently admonished me by saying that if I had been God I would have carved 'Jesus Saves' into the bark of every tree.

Apparently the Master Designer was more subtle than I had acknowledged him to be. He knew how to sparingly use brilliant mauves and oranges, both in quantity and in length of time. There was such a thing as good taste and God had it. Life was not all glorious sunsets. There were grey days as well—at least in England there were—and the greys were all different shades. Nick liked to see the clouds rushing across the sky with creative excitement and even purported to appreciate the foreboding brought by a heavy grey day.

Hmmm! Well that is what we got for our weekend away. That plus driving rain at times.

Somehow the man had got through to me and I set off deciding to enjoy the weekend whatever the weather, instead of moaning continually. I think I actually embraced the foul day!

As the rain splattered through the nearly closed window I found to my surprise it was most refreshing. Thankfully the clouds did not sit on top of my head and bring on depression, but hurried across the sky.

We togged ourselves up to brave the elements and strode the length of Dovedale before retiring to our hotel for a good bath, a change of clothes and a hot meal.

It was one of the most enjoyable and memorable weekends we have ever experienced. And it could all have been wasted.

Puddles

I was delighted to hear from a young lady in East Kent who heard me speak at a conference in the Romford area in Essex.

She told how she felt so liberated from legalism, so set free from having to be a good Christian and live up to standards, that the next day when she woke up and saw it was pouring with rain, she put on her wellingtons and went up the village street stamping in all the puddles.

Her godly simplicity and childlike approach to life had always appealed to me. Now her act of uninhibited liberty rebounded as a challenge to me to live the life I spoke about by choice, not because I should.

I have always envied Alan from Hemel, who recently said, 'How good it is to be carefree enough to run a stick along the railings just like we did when we were kids' . . . and he is only sixty-five at the time of writing.

I am afraid I have always been a natural worrier myself. But thankfully I do not worry that I am worried, for I have nothing to prove!

I'm OK.

Flower Power

'Faithful in little, faithful in much' has always been a favourite little verse of mine. Never more graphically expressed than one mid-week lunch-hour after two of us had spoken and sung to some prosperous-looking businessmen in the City of London.

As they went back to their desks and phones my friend and I walked to Liverpool Street Station. We passed a very old lady selling newspapers outside an Underground station and walked on enjoying the sunshine. Something seemed to be troubling my friend and a hundred yards on he suddenly stopped and said, 'Hold my guitar a moment will you?' and dashed back down the street.

Peering through all the pavement hoppers I saw him enter a florist's and emerge with a huge bunch of flowers which he gave to the old lady. It was a lovely touch.

'Couldn't help it,' he said later, 'Just had to do it!'

When I asked he told me she was overcome.

I am not surprised.

Oh, isn't it just the little things?

Wives Know Best

In early charismatic days I was a well-known public speaker and we always gave the impression we had our act together.

In a crowded room I passed my wife talking to a very spiritual-looking lady. She did not see me and as I brushed past I heard this admirer saying, 'It must be wonderful to be married to Maurice Smith!'

She had obviously seen me as a tiny figure on large platforms, heard my pearls of wisdom and assumed this made me a model Christian husband.

I hurried on before I heard my wife's answer. She knows the truth. I feel sure Eileen does not want to divorce me, but—'wonderful'? A bit over the top I would say.

I wonder what she said? That was twenty years ago and I have never asked her. What am I afraid of?